Frankie

Mrs. R. D. Randolph
and Texas Liberal Politics

by
Ann Fears Crawford

EAKIN PRESS ⬥ Austin, Texas

FIRST EDITION

Copyright © 2000
By Ann Fears Crawford

Published in the United States of America
By Eakin Press
A Division of Sunbelt Media, Inc.
P.O. Drawer 90159 ⬥ Austin, Texas 78709-0159
email: eakinpub@sig.net
⬛ website: www.eakinpress.com ⬛

1   2   3   4   5   6   7   8   9

1-57168-351-8

Library of Congress Cataloging-in-Publication Data

Crawford, Ann Fears
   Frankie: Mrs. R. D. Randolph and Texas liberal politics / by Ann Fears Crawford—
1st ed.
      p.   cm.
   Includes bibliographical references and index.
   ISBN 1-57168-351-8
   1. Randolph, Frankie Carter, 1894-1972. 2. Women politicians—Texas—Biography. 3.
Politicians—Texas—Biography. 4. Texas—Politics and government, 1951–. 5.
Democratic Party (Tex.)—Biography. 6. Liberalism—Texas—History—20th century.
I. Title.
F391.4.R36 C73   1999
324.2764'06'092--dc21
   [B]   99-052369

For Callie
and Billie and Molly, who carry the torch,
and in grateful memory of
Fagan Dickson and Robert Morse Crunden

Frankie Carter Randolph
  —Texas Observer

Contents

Foreword

"Never underestimate how an exemplary life can
persist in the imagination of others. How it can
inspire beyond death."

— Ariel Dorfman

    The words of the Chilean poet Ariel Dorfman seem partic-
ularly apt to the life of Frankie Randolph. The book you are
about to read is filled with interviews and insights of those who
knew Frankie Randolph personally, who worked with her, and
who acknowledged her courage and fortitude.

    I, on the other hand, and many of my contemporaries who
followed her, gained so much from her exemplary life. During
my first term in the Texas House of Representatives, I began
coming to Houston to discuss what was happening in the Texas
legislature. I was asked to do this by my fellow legislators who
were members of the Harris County Democrats, and I continued to update legislative activities during the "Dirty Thirty" days
of 1971.

    I quickly recognized how easily I, as a woman in the House
of Representatives, was accepted by the group, but at that time,
I did not know the source of this acceptance. The Harris County
Democrats was the only group I spoke before in Texas where the

issue of my being a woman did not come up. There was an acceptance among this group that was extraordinarily refreshing.

Now, reviewing Frankie Randolph's life and what she meant to the Harris County Democrats and liberal Democrats across the state, I realize that this acceptance was a direct result of her labors. She led politicians to realize that they could actually work side-by-side with a woman in the political arena.

The value of Ann's book is that it retrieves this wonderful woman's life and the times she lived in and gives them to us for our times and for posterity. The book is filled with the extraordinary words of Texans who shared firsthand experiences with Mrs. Randolph. The chief attributes that characterize this remarkable woman are her courage, her independence, and her steadfastness.

Those who knew her and worked with her in politics had the benefit of that direct knowledge. They had that knowledge to inspire them and to work for them through the Harris County Democrats.

Then there were other women, and I include myself among those, who have entered political life and have faced seemingly insurmountable barriers. Those people who worked with Frankie Randolph, who were touched by her political fervor, learned to have an acceptance of women in the political arena. This acceptance was invaluable to those of us who came after her.

Mrs. Randolph helped send Harris County Democrats to the Texas legislature. In the 1970s many of them became my political *compadres*. She educated many of them in liberal issues, and throughout her life educated herself on national issues. Hers was never a static life. She kept moving forward and kept enlarging not only her horizons, but the horizons of those she worked with.

Frankie Randolph was an educator, an organizer, and we are so fortunate in having her lasting legacy, the *Texas Observer*. What would we do without it?

— Frances "Sissy" Farenthold
Houston, Texas
September 1999

Preface

*W*riting *Frankie: Mrs. R. D. Randolph and Texas Liberal Politics* has been a labor of love. Since the late 1950s, Frankie Randolph has been a fascinating figure to me, a "mover and shaker" in the world of Texas politics in an age when few women were leaders in the political arena and those who voted wore hats and white gloves.

I first glimpsed her during one of her famous "rump" sessions, sitting stoically in a folding chair under an umbrella, filled with umbrage and disgust with those she considered traitors to the Democratic party.

I wanted to know all about her, and there was much to learn. Fortunately, there was the *Texas Observer*, carrying news stories and editorials detailing the doings of the liberal-loyalists, who stood in opposition to the Shivercrats. And fortunately there were the writings of Ronnie Dugger and Willie Morris to sing the praises of Randolph, the guiding spirit behind the *Texas Observer*.

The 1950s and 1960s were turbulent times in which the state was shaking off its rural, agricultural roots and moving toward becoming an urban, industrial state, whose politicians were major players on the national scene. However, civil rights and issues related to a changing nation and world were causing many politicians to look for change. Others, including Dixie-crats and Shivercrats, worked avidly to maintain the *status quo*.

Texans Sam Rayburn and Lyndon Johnson were reputed to be in full control of the Democratic party, with John Connally working behind the scenes for Johnson. And then there was Allan Shivers. Growing up in Beaumont, Texas, I learned that Shivers was the most promising politician to come from the area since William P. Hobby left as editor of the *Beaumont Enterprise* to become the state's lieutenant governor.

What then were the roots of the split within the Democratic party? How did a society matron from Houston, Texas, come to play such an important role in the liberal-loyalist politics of the times?

Many of my questions were answered when I explored Texas politics during the 1950s and 1960s for my dissertation, "John B. Connally: The Making of a Governor." Conversations with Robert Caro when he was in Texas researching the formative years of Lyndon Johnson added to my fascination with Frankie Randolph. Any woman who could go "eyeball to eyeball" with Lyndon and win had my vote.

Two other historians, George Green and Don Carleton, were also researching the role of liberals and the politics of the era. Their works aided enormously in an understanding of the times and the issues that split the Democratic party in Texas between conservatives and labor-loyalists.

In the late 1980s, when my colleague Crystal Ragsdale and I were putting together the entries for our second book together, *Texas Women: Frontier to Future*, Frankie Randolph headed the list. Both Crystal and I had been involved in liberal politics from the late 1950s and knew of Frankie Randolph and her work with the labor-loyalists. We had both worked assiduously under the direction of Jean Lee, another superb Texas political woman, to help send Maury Maverick, Jr., to the Texas House of Representatives, and we knew the hard political row liberals had to hoe during this period.

Then the research began, and Ed Cogburn warned me, "Don't write a word until you've talked to Billie." Sage advice from one of the masters of liberal politics in Harris County. Billie Carr gave me insights into Randolph, answered many questions, and posed even more.

Researching the life of Frankie Randolph has been an adventure. The road from pineywoods girlhood to liberal politics was not hard for me to imagine, for I had taken the same route. Seeking out the answers to Randolph's developing sense of social justice and her political philosophy, however, has been an endlessly fascinating quest.

At one point my research associate, J. Ramsey Sutter, noted: "You don't want just to write about Randolph, you want to BE her." Maybe so. But then Frankie Randolph was *sui generis*—the right woman in the right place at the right time. And that place and time was Texas liberal politics during the 1950s and 1960s.

Here is her story.

Acknowledgments

*W*hen I began researching and writing the full-fledged biography of Frankie Randolph, I knew there would be problems in gathering primary source material. In writing the vignette on Randolph for *Texas Women: Frontier to Future*, I was told by Billie Carr that Randolph had the habit of reading letters from such notable political figures as Adlai Stevenson and Ralph Yarborough and then tearing them in half and discarding them.

Without the help of Billie Carr and Randolph's granddaughter, Molly Luhrs, few primary source materials would be available to the biographer. Molly simply handed to me all the papers available, with the exception of those she had already donated to the Woodson Research Center, Fondren Library, Rice University. Nancy Booth, head of Special Collections at Rice, and her staff were most patient with my numerous visits to use Randolph's papers there, as well as the papers of Walter Hall and Fagan Dickson.

In addition to Nancy and her staff, Will Howard and the staff of the Texas Room, Houston Public Library, helped with research into the politics and social life of Houston, while Ralph Elder and the staff of the Center for American History, University of Texas at Austin, aided with additional research. The entire staff of the *Texas Observer* was most generous in aiding with both articles and photographs, and the *Texas Observer* remains the best source for the politics of the period.

Bernard Rapoport, that most gracious and generous of Texans, first suggested that I use Frankie Randolph as the focal point for the politics of the 1950s and 1960s, and, as always, his judgment was sound. My very dear friend Nadine Eckhardt spent endless hours locating people involved in Texas politics during the period and setting up interviews for me. Believe me, if you are lost in the sixties, Nadine can find you.

When I made an appointment to interview Kathleen Voight, a political contemporary of Randolph's, she made a comment concerning the leaders of the labor-loyalist movement of the 1940s and 1950s. "We started and we've never wavered from our goal," she told me, and I found that her memories, along with those of Eddie Ball, Chris Dixie, and Creekmore Fath, were fresh and clear. They are wonderful sources and true political leaders.

Former Congressman Bob Eckhardt and J. Edwin Smith shared their memories of the Harris County Democrats and the fight to send liberals to the Texas legislature, while another good friend, Bill Kilgarlin, shared his adventures and knowledge of their campaign efforts.

I spent an enjoyable afternoon listening to Lida Edmundson and George Anna Lucas Burke recall the involvement of Frankie Randolph in the Junior League and the social life of Houston, and an equally wonderful evening with my friend, Texas historian George Green, "talking labor."

The archivists at the John Gray Library, Lamar University, Beaumont, were helpful in locating materials on the East Texas lumber industry, while the archivists at the Anderson archives, M.D. Anderson Library, University of Houston, aided with materials on Houston politics and the Harris County Democrats. Bill Hord and Joe Washburn, librarians at Houston Community College, saw that books and articles on the politics of the period were instantly available when I needed them.

I would never have realized the importance of Frankie Randolph without the articles of three friends writing for the *Texas Observer*. Willie Morris, Ronnie Dugger, and Molly Ivins turned

Texans on to this remarkable woman and kept her memory fresh. In the late 1950s, another of the *Observer* crowd, Larry Goodwyn, set my feet on the path with his wise words: "Stop fooling around—write politics," while the late Robert M. Crunden, professor of American Studies, University of Texas at Austin, provided the intellectual impetus to expand my views on Texas politics.

My colleagues John Ben and J. Ramsey Sutter are always ready to indulge in conversations on Texas liberal politics, while Jack Keever is always there to be sure that what I write makes good sense and good politics. My administrative assistant, Felicia Vega, has had a two-year education in "Frankie," keeping the files and interviews straight, while my publisher, Ed Eakin, knew from the beginning that the book on Randolph was an important one and that I was the one to write it.

Longtime friends Donnette Moss, Pat Wright, and Jane Tullos provided bed and board while I researched politics in Austin and San Antonio.

The greatest debt of gratitude that I owe is to two people who early in my teaching career helped to form my political philosophy. When as a speech teacher in Beaumont, Texas, I was assigned a debate topic dealing with the legality of labor unions, I asked G. E. Hatton, Sr. to tell me all about unions and their goals. He flatly refused, telling me that I had to experience unions and union issues firsthand. He allowed me to tag along to meetings in his CIO union hall, and I became a labor-liberal for life.

During my years in Austin, Fagan Dickson enlightened me on many of the important liberal issues, both on the state and the national scene. I count our conversations as some of the most significant in my life. Fagan also allowed me to sit in on his conversations with the courtly and erudite Major Jubal R. Parten. Their views and their discussions were memorable.

All of these—and more—have helped to make this book come alive. I am everlastingly grateful.

ONE

Pineywoods Girlhood

The world in which Frankie Carter was born on January 25, 1894, was an endlessly wondrous and fascinating one. The East Texas pineywoods, encompassing more than 36,000 square miles and lying between the Post Oak and Backland Prairie and the Texas Coastal Plain, were impressive even to the earliest settlers coming into Texas.

Stephen F. Austin foresaw the commercial possibilities of the area watered by the Sabine, Neches, Trinity, and San Jacinto rivers with its lush, almost overpowering forests composed of pine and other hardwoods. He prophesied that among the "staple industries of Texas would be lumber."

Other visitors to the area caught the splendor of the pineywoods with its stands of longleaf pines, their massive trunks measuring four to five feet in diameter, their magnificent limbs soaring 100 to 150 feet in the air. With its fertile, sandy soil, numerous waterways, and long growing season, East Texas, an extension of the southern pine forests that swept westward from Georgia, provided a glimpse of home to settlers pushing into Texas from the Cotton South.

Pine trees, including the massive longleaf, shortleaf, and

loblolly, intermixed with oak, birch, ash, and sweet gum, plus the lordly cypress growing in and along the waterways, were the sentinels of the forests, beckoning travelers in the East Texas region to settle there. And they came in droves, lured by fertile soil, good climate, and cheap land, giving to the area its distinct Southern culture. They built homes among the pines and moss-bearded oaks, built towns along the waterways, and soon embarked on business ventures. And the most lucrative business of all would be timber.

From the early days of the Republic of Texas, when Andrew Smyth and other East Texas rivermen harvested the hard-woods, floating them on keelboats from Bevilport to Sabine Pass and then moving them overland to the burgeoning town of Beaumont, timber was the focus of commercial enterprise. By the 1850s, steamboats plied the Sabine, Neches, Trinity, Red, and Angelina rivers, carrying lumber, while port towns were growing, among them Jefferson on the Red River and Sabine Pass at the mouth of the Sabine.

Mary Austin Holley, cousin of Stephen F. Austin and one of the first promoters of Texas, predicted that "fortunes may be realized by good sawyers, with slight capital," a call that resonated among Texas entrepreneurs, eager to make their fortunes in the new republic.

By the end of the 1830s, Robert Wilson had established one of the first steam sawmills near Harrisburg on Buffalo Bayou, followed by Robert Booth and Robert Jackson's steam sawmills near Orange. These early mills were built around the sash saw, "a single sawblade . . . [that] cut only on the downstroke." The high-speed circular saw was yet to come.

By 1860, despite treacherous rivers often flooded by spring rains, and horrendous travel conditions along almost non-existent Texas roads, Texas claimed approximately two hundred sawmills, employing almost twelve hundred workers. Builders in the North and East scoffed at yellow pine, deeming it inferior, but with the steady demand for housing and depletion of the great white pine forests in the North, the era of East Texas long-leaf yellow pine, manifesting great strength and flexibility, was soon to come.

Following the path of the pine forests from Georgia to Texas were the Carters, who would become members of the "East Texas aristocracy," the timber barons making their fortunes from the virgin pines of East Texas. Young Frankie could look back to a family intimately involved in Texas lumbering since its inception.

Joseph John Carter, born in Newton County, Georgia, on July 17, 1826, began lumbering in Cherokee County, Texas, well before the Civil War. However, when war broke out, Carter served as captain of a group of volunteers, part of Hubbard's regiment, under the command of his nephew, Col. Richard B. Hubbard. He donated all the steel from his sawmill to his regiment for armament production.

After the war, Carter returned to stave making on land near Huntington in Angelina County. He had married Jane Eleanor Agnes Anderson, whose father died in Georgia, leaving a substantial inheritance. In 1870 Carter's son, Joseph John, then only seventeen, traveled from Texas to Georgia and brought back his mother's share of the estate—six thousand dollars in gold—safely stored in his belt.

A princely sum for the time, this inheritance was used by Carter to make a cash payment on land, machinery, and equipment to establish the first sawmill on the Oretega Grant in Trinity County. In 1876, when J. J. Carter failed to complete his payments for the machinery and equipment, his creditors foreclosed, and the property was bought at sale by Col. Sam T. Robb, a prominent attorney, who then conveyed the property to J. J.'s third son, twenty-year-old William Thomas.

Born in Tyler, Texas, on February 4, 1856, W. T. Carter operated the mill at its original site for a time. In the later years of the nineteenth century, before the railroad had penetrated the pineywoods, it was more economical to move the sawmill to the timber than to haul timber to the mill, and so Carter moved the mill several times, following the timber.

While a young student at the Steele Academy in Pennington, W. T. Carter had met Maude Holley, who had been born in Marion, Alabama, and had come to Texas with her parents. Porter Jackson Holley had made farming his business, and had done well in Texas. Maude's mother, Frank Matthews Holley, was said to be a "great beauty," and Maude would name her youngest daughter after her. Maude and W. T. began courting during their schooldays, and on January 16, 1879, Maude's twenty-first birthday, the couple were married. Throughout his lifetime, W. T. often teased his wife: "Maude, you know you tricked me into marrying you; you were the only girl I couldn't kiss, and in order to enjoy this privilege, you enticed me into matrimony...." Nevertheless, W. T. often boasted that marrying Maude was "the finest investment he ever made."

While W. T. was building his lumber business, Maude began the careful rearing of their children. Lena Lister was born on November 24, 1879, followed by Jessie Gertrude on April 19, 1881.

In 1882 W. T. purchased a mill and timber holdings in Polk County at Barnum, but fire destroyed the first mill there. The fire wreaked havoc on the family life of W. T. and Maude as well. While the mill was being rebuilt and a home built for the family, W. T. sent his wife and the two children to stay with her parents on their farm near Trinity.

For some weeks, Maude endured being separated from her husband and not being there to follow the progress of the new mill. Then she sent a note to her husband: "Willy. The children and I are arriving by flat-car two weeks from today; please find some place for us to live—a good clean tent will do."

"Willy" turned to an admiring neighbor, Mrs. Hammond, and arranged to rent the spare room in her house for his family. On a cold winter's day, Maude, with hot bricks at her feet and her children snuggled in blankets, mounted the "chairs on a flat car" and began her journey. Her husband met the family at Corrigan, and they spent the night there. Then it was home to spend time in Mrs. Hammond's log cabin until their house was finished.

The new mill required capital, and legend circulated among the lumber workers that W. T. financed the new mill by selling his horse for $35. Realizing the need for extended management, in 1882 W. T. and his brother Ernest, who had been working at the mill, organized W. T. Carter & Bro., with another partner, A. B. Caton, who later sold his participating interest to the other partners.

In 1887 Lizzie Carter, the wife of W. T.'s brother Ernest, died giving birth to a son, whom Ernest named William Thomas, for his brother. Young Willie was taken into the family of Maude and W. T., eventually upon his father's death was adopted by them, and was treated just as if he were their own child. As W. T.'s business expanded, so did his and Maude's brood, with the births of Agnese Jayne, August 4, 1889, Aubrey Leon, June 17, 1892, and their last child, Frankie, January 25, 1894.

In August 1897 a neighbor spotted billows of smoke coming from the Barnum mill. People from the surrounding area rushed to put out the flames, but, filled with extremely flammable lumber, the mill burned to the ground. Lacking sufficient funds to rebuild, W. T. would have to borrow from Houston banks. He decided to move the mill to a site seven miles east of Moscow. Maude gave the new company town its name—Camden.

Camden became one of the mill towns that dotted the East Texas pineywoods, and life for the lumber workers centered around the town. For seventy years, the company town flourished, with millworkers paying only a few dollars for homes built by the Carters. If a worker died, the widow and children continued to live in the house; the company never evicted anyone.

The center of the company town was a boardinghouse, where single lumber workers, who often moved from milltown to milltown, could stay and board, drawing their pay at the company commissary. Camden had the distinction of being the last of the East Texas company towns, with its boardinghouse turning out good food for boarders and visitors until the mill was sold in 1968 to U.S. Plywood, a subsidiary of Champion Paper.

Getting lumber from the woodlands to markets continued to be a problem, and in May 1898 W. T. and other investors incorporated the Moscow, Camden, and San Augustine, a shortline railway running sixty-five miles from Moscow to San Augustine. On November 19, 1898, Carter extended the line to the new sawmill at Camden. At Moscow the railway connected with the Houston, East and West Texas, which later changed its name to Texas and New Orleans, and even later to Southern Pacific.

The railway changed its name to "railroad" in the 1920s, but to many of the millworkers in and around Camden, MC&SA

meant "Mr. Carter's and Sid Adams's Railroad," after W. T. and his mill superintendent. The "archetypical southern short-line mixed train," the MC&SA often carried passengers from Camden to Moscow to shop for items not available in the company store, but the railroad never did extend to San Augustine.

No tickets were sold for this railroad; passengers merely got on the train, handed their quarter for a one-way trip to conductor Carl Vincent, and went to Moscow. The fare was raised to fifty cents in 1971. The train also carried the mail, and riding the train from Camden to Moscow became a delight for many East Texans.

In the 1960s, with East Texas increasingly becoming a tourist attraction, the MC&SA, equipped with a diesel engine, but still with its oldtime rattan passenger seats, took tourists on a leisurely one-and-one-half-hour ride over creeks and lakes through the scenic pineywoods. It was not until July 9, 1973, that the passenger train was discontinued, but Engine No. 5 of the MC&SA remains a tourist attraction, sitting across from the Polk County Museum and Library in Livingston, Texas, a steadfast symbol of the days when a whistle in the pineywoods meant the MC&SA was on its way, carrying lumber from East Texas to the markets of the world.

While W. T. developed his timber business, Maude Carter taught their children their "ABCs." Soon the couple realized that they would need help with educating their children. W. T. added a schoolroom to the house, and Margie Day from Huntsville was engaged full-time to teach the growing Carter brood.

But life was not all school and church. The East Texas pineywoods, where the Carter clan lived, was one of nature's wonderlands, a land where children could run wild, swing from trees, picnic, and take part in fish fries and watermelon parties. There were berries to be picked (mayhaw, blackberry, and dewberry), and fruit to be gathered from the peach, pear, and plum trees so that Maude and her household helpers could turn them into jellies and preserves for the table.

Young Frankie and her sisters would peek around trees, watching with envy from the side of the bank, while their brothers swung from ropes into the cool, clear water of the creeks. Girls were not allowed to shed their petticoats and skirts to plunge into creekbottoms or even to lift their skirts to splash along the sandbars.

Each season brought a round of activities for the children to enjoy. In the fall there were nuts, black walnuts and chinquapins, to gather if one wanted Christmas cakes, while the making of cane syrup was an adventure to catch any child's imagination. A yoked cow walked in circles all day powering a crude machine that extracted juice from the cane. Then the juice was boiled in black kettles until it achieved the proper consistency for pure ribbon cane, the "sweetnin'" of East Texas.

The first frost was "hog-killin' time," eagerly awaited by W. T. Carter, who prided himself on his sausage making. He carefully measured so much fat, so much lean, just the right amount of seasoning, and then packed the sausage into casings made from the pig's intestines. Sausage links took a place of honor in the smokehouse, along with hams and bacons. One worker sat up all night to make sure the hickory sticks were kept smoldering for proper curing. Then the Carter girls would gather around the kitchen table, while Maude and her workers prepared chitterlings and pickled souse from the feet, ears, and head of the pig.

Winter was the time to shell nuts for Christmas desserts, play games, and take part in singsongs and "socials." Christmas was a glorious event in East Texas families, with its tree hauled to the house, simple presents shared, and weeks spent preparing a wealth of delicacies for Christmas dinner.

Maude Carter's responsibilities were not limited to teaching her children kitchen skills and the rudiments of education. One of her "fields of endeavor," according to her daughter Agnese, was helping each child to develop a "social conscience." Like many East Texas women, during a time when professional help was in short supply, Maude was called on to care for the sick, often served as midwife, and helped prepare bodies for burial.

Maude taught her children the "responsibility of helping people less fortunate than we were." This sense of responsibility to society, instilled by their mother, would result in each of the daughters benefiting society in her own special way.

Lena, the eldest, would devote her time and efforts to the organization and management of the Young Women's Christian Association in Houston, and Agnese, "moved by the population explosion" in the lives of families where "children were not wanted and would not be cared for," helped organize Houston's Planned Parenthood. Jessie, who according to Agnese was "the most magnanimous of us," always had "an open purse" and encouraged her husband, Dr. Judson Taylor, to give half his time to providing medical care for those who could not afford it.

And it was the early influence of Maude Carter that would foster her youngest daughter Frankie's desire to work for civil rights and to "get fair play for the neglected voters of Harris County."

TWO

From Houston Hoyden to Society Matron

The twentieth century brought significant changes in the life of the Carter family, and Frankie, as the youngest child, was profoundly affected by these changes. W. T. Carter was "always a keen, interested sawmill man who liked to direct his own lumber making operations," and was often seen clad in an undershirt, "sweat on his brow and grease on his hands," directing the repair of a piece of machinery.

By 1903, however, with his timber business prospering, W. T. had made his fortune, and the city of Houston beckoned. By the turn of the century, timber baron John Henry Kirby had already moved his lumbering headquarters to the city that was a thriving rail center linking Southeast Texas to the cotton, timber, and cattle producing areas of the state.

Carter was drawn to Houston, as well, and moved his family into a mansion at 2310 Main Street, the city's main thorough-fare. The older girls were delighted with the mansion's ballroom, where they could entertain their friends at formal dances, but the stables were the main attraction for teenage Frankie. She rode as often as possible, becoming an avid horsewoman, a pursuit she continued after her marriage.

Even with the move, W. T. remained actively involved in the lumber business, building a new steel-and-concrete timber mill, in the wake of yet another fire, and moving the general sales office of W. T. Carter & Bro. to the city in 1910. By that year the Carters had become noted members of the Houston social scene, and W. T. reigned as King Nottoc XII (cotton spelled backward) at the city's Nu-Tsu-Oh (Houston spelled backward) Carnival.

By 1919, however, he was ready to relinquish the business, turning the management of the timber operations over to his son Aubrey, who had recently returned from serving as an air force pilot in World War I, while W. T., Jr., took over the management of the family investment and real-estate holdings.

Prior to relinquishing control of the business, W. T. and Maude distributed the majority of their estate to their six children. According to his daughter Agnese, W. T. wanted to "watch out for any mistakes his children would make and help them with his counsel." In addition, in 1913 the graduated income tax had been passed, and he was hoping to avoid any further gift and inheritance taxes on his estate.

The timber business continued to prosper. In 1922 a hardwood mill with a single-band saw, dry kilns, cooling sheds, and drying yards was added about a half mile away from the pine plant in Camden. A modern planing mill was added later.

Despite the amenities of the house on Main, the Carters were soon to make a move, creating a family enclave at Houston's exclusive Courtlandt Place. Laid out in 1907 and located between Westmoreland and Avondale streets, Courtlandt Place would become the scene of many Carter family gatherings and festivities. C. L. Neuhaus built the subdivision's first house, Number 6, in 1906, and with his marriage to Lillie Neuhaus, W. T. Carter, Jr., established his home at Number 18.

Houston architect Birdsall Briscoe, who would design many of the homes of Courtlandt Place, planned the interiors of Number 16 for Lena and her husband, James J. Carroll, and designed a home at Number 20 for Jessie and her husband, Dr. Judson Taylor. No doubt feeling family pressure, W. T. charged Briscoe to design a home at Number 14 for him, Maude, son

Aubrey, and Frankie. W. T. would die on February 23, 1921, before the home's completion, but Maude would live there throughout her life. Aubrey would marry in the front parlor to Marjorie Leachman. Frankie would live there before her marriage to R. D. Randolph in 1918, and the young couple would make their home there after their marriage.

School and social activities were very much a part of the Carter family's lifestyle, but Frankie was rebellious about both. Whether the move from East Texas upset her expectations of life and her sense of security or whether she could simply never settle down to school is difficult to assess. However, she made failing grades in many of her classes and was never a satisfactory student.

Wanting to assure his daughter's education, W. T. hired a tutor for her. Willie Hutcheson was to have a profound effect on Frankie's education and her growing sense of social justice. A divorced woman who took back her maiden name, Hutcheson smoked cigars and embarked on a career as the music critic for the *Houston Post*. She was one of the original founders of the Woman's Choral Club, and one of the growing group of "woman scribblers" who invaded the world of journalism in the twentieth century.

Getting Frankie to write must have been a challenge even for the formidable Hutcheson. Under her tutor's watchful eye, Frankie began an ambitious study project in American history in an accounting ledger book. She listed the various countries settling America, and the beginning colonies; however, she never continued her work beyond the Revolutionary period.

Nevertheless, Hutcheson was an inspiring teacher, instilling in her young charge a sense of history, helping discipline the young woman's mind, and continuing the lessons in social justice begun by Maude Carter.

There were lessons to be learned from her father also. W. T. was an ardent admirer of Woodrow Wilson, and he would often spend time during dinner, with his entire family gathered around the table, discussing politics and the events of the day. As a young woman, Frankie must have listened avidly to W. T.'s stories of Wilson's rise to power as a progressive governor of New

Jersey, his reaching the presidency with the aid of Texan Edward Mandell House and his "crowd" of determined Democrats.

No doubt W. T. regaled his family with stories of Texas's "Immortal Forty," the Democratic delegates who held the floor for Wilson during his initial bid for the presidency, and the entrance of numbers of Texas Democrats into positions of leadership during Wilson's administration.

Despite the attempts of Hutcheson and of her father to make Frankie a student, however, she became what would be known today as a rebellious teenager. Frankie's teenage years coincided with the introduction of the automobile into American life, and Houstonians were embarking on their love affair with the automobile. By 1906, when Frankie was twelve, the city had eighty automobiles and an Automobile Club, composed of sixty-one devotees.

As a teenager, Frankie coaxed her brother Aubrey into teaching her to drive and practiced her driving skills following in the ruts of the lumber trucks in Camden. Becoming a skilled driver, she could often be glimpsed behind the wheel of the family roadster, careening down Main Street. Her aunt fainted dead away when she heard of Frankie's daredevil adventures.

Despite her adventures at the wheel of the roadster, Frankie continued to perform flamboyant acts on horseback. When she was fifteen, she was once stopped by police for wearing her brother's shoulder holster and pistol while galloping her horse through Houston's Hermann Park. No doubt Frankie thought she was celebrating Texas's western heritage. Her hoydenish ways would become legend among family members and her political friends. According to Billie Carr, the impetuous Frankie was "churched," kicked out of the Baptist church for dancing.

And dancing was very much a part of her social activities. Each year in November, Houston continued to celebrate its No-Tsu-Oh Carnival, paying homage to its chief export—cotton. For six days the city reveled in flower-bedecked floats carrying young women in ornate costumes, band music, and the coronation of its king.

On November 8, 1914, the *Daily Post* carried the announcement of the year's festivities: "All Readiness for Houston's

Jubilee," and King Nottoc ceded his throne to King Retaw I (water spelled backward), and at the end of the festivities, King Retaw I, Eugene Arthur Hudson, crowned Frankie Carter as his queen. How the newly crowned queen felt about her ornate satin gown and headdress has not been recorded, but her grand-daughter Molly remembered that Frankie never felt comfortable in fancy dress.

The focus from cotton to water reflected the growing importance of the Port of Houston to the city, and Queen Frankie and King Retaw I celebrated the opening of the completed Ship Channel. Houston, however, was to celebrate only one more No-Tsu-Oh Carnival, in 1915. With World War I a reality in Europe, Texans, along with other Americans, turned their thoughts to the war effort. Somewhat reluctantly, Frankie Carter turned her thoughts to completing her studies at Baldwin School for Girls in Bryn Mawr, Pennsylvania.

With her brother, Aubrey, at the nearby University of Virginia, Frankie was often included in social events. The most memorable event of her finishing school days was undoubtedly when Aubrey introduced her to fellow student Robert Decan Randolph, a descendant of the Randolphs, who were among the first families of Virginia.

"Deke" Randolph's mother, Jane, was related through her Diehl side of the family to Marguerite Radclyffe Hall. While in her twenties, Hall visited Washington and became fascinated with the widowed Jane, who was ten years her senior. She began a love affair with her. Hall would later become an accomplished poet and novelist, writing, in 1928, *The Well of Loneliness*, the most notorious novel of lesbian life of the first part of the twentieth century. She would write of Jane's "perfect figure, lovely hands and feet and masses of long and beautiful auburn hair."

The two women embarked on a madcap adventure, touring the South in an old jalopy. Subsequently, Hall swooped up Jane and her children, taking them back to England to live with her grandmother, while she and Jane continued their love affair. Eventually, Jane married a Texan, Harry Caruth, and the Randolph clan moved back to America. However, during the war years, Jane's son, Deke, visited with Marguerite Radclyffe Hall while on a tour of duty in England, and his sister, Winifred, corresponded with the writer throughout the 1920s.

With World War I and the trenches of France calling America's young men, Deke was one of the first to enlist, training for the fledgling Naval Air Corps in Canada. He soloed after only ninety minutes of instruction in the air and promptly crash landed. Nevertheless, he qualified as an aviator cadet, received Navy pilot license Number 165, and helped design the official "Navy Wings." Before leaving for service in France, he visited Frankie in Houston.

Members of Houston's young set were saying tearful good-byes at ice-cream socials and yachting parties, and fun-loving Frankie often attended with Mike Hogg, who would also soon be in uniform. On one boating excursion, Deke Randolph fell overboard, and Frankie dived in after him. Mike Hogg knew his days as Frankie's suitor were doomed and simply gave up.

Perhaps Frankie and Deke decided to marry before he left for France or shortly after he returned. One week before they married, "Frank," as he called her, wired him in Washington that all plans were set and she was off for the weekend at Galveston's famed Galvez Hotel. The couple were married on June 14, 1918, in a large, formal wedding which Frankie was persuaded to have. In all the wedding photographs, her granddaughter recalled, she "looks madder than hell."

While Frankie began the life of a typical Houston society matron, Deke entered the brokerage business, then went to East Texas to work for the Carter Lumber Company. In 1924 he also helped with the Carter Investment Company and was elected to the board of directors of Union National Bank. The banking business fascinated him, and he entered banking full-time in 1947, as executive vice-president and trust officer of Union National Bank. In 1958 he was elected senior vice-president of Texas National Bank, a position he would hold throughout his lifetime.

Frankie and Deke lived first in the house at Courtlandt Place, which she inherited from her mother. Then, tiring of maintaining such a large establishment, they lived in apartments for a number of years. They eventually moved to a three-bedroom home at 3726 Meadow Lake Lane in River Oaks, taking with them many of the furnishings and paintings from the Carter home at Courtlandt Place. To Frankie, the "simple, convenient, one-level house" would be her home for many years.

While Deke pursued his career interests, Frankie busied herself with the life of a society matron, but one with a purpose. In the wake of the progressive era, with its focus on club women working as volunteers for the betterment of their communities, a group of Houston women came together to establish a chapter of the Junior League. When she heard about the possibility of forming a chapter of the national group, Frankie said, "I don't know what a Junior League is, but let's do it." And do it they did.

In 1924 twelve Houston women met at the home of Mrs. Luke C. Bradley to form the Houston chapter, and among the twelve founding members was Frankie Randolph. She would serve as the league's second president in 1925-26. The group elected officers, discussed a project to raise funds for their efforts, and decided the causes they would support. Although an article in the national league's magazine noted that the purpose of the new chapter was to "train debutantes to combine a gay and happy life with a life of usefulness," Houston members remember that their work with the league led to a lifetime commitment to community.

Looking for a way to finance their programs, the league members determined to open a Luncheon Club in the basement of the Gibralter Building at San Jacinto and Capitol, a building owned by W. T. Carter, Jr. Frankie recalled that W. T. told them "he had all the room in the world in the basement, so we took it over." The husbands scoffed at the idea, saying that "nobody ever made money selling food, especially one meal a day. It was impossible!" However, the league members persisted, talked their husbands, brothers, and friends into having lunch at the club, and volunteered to do the cooking, serve the lunches, and clean up after the lunch hour. Soon the club was a huge success, and the league members had funds to embark on their community projects.

Public health was of great concern during this period before free clinics, and the focus of the league members was the health of their city's mothers and children. Armed with funds from their Luncheon Club, the women opened a clinic devoted to prenatal and children's health in the First National Bank Building. Doctors volunteered their time to give immunizations and free dental care to needy children. The clinic was such a success that it later moved to Hermann Hospital as a "well-baby" clinic and then to Texas Children's Hospital as the Junior League Outpatient Clinic.

Although Frankie Randolph took her league activities very seriously, she never missed an opportunity to be outside or to engage in sports. Along with a dedicated group of women golfers, a new sporting diversion for women, she could be seen swinging her club on a nine-hole course behind Jeff Davis Hospital. She strolled onto the links clad in a striped ankle-length skirt, a white shirt and tie, jacket, high-topped boots, and a snap-brimmed Panama hat. The women golfers eventually moved to the Houston Golf Club, which became the Houston Country Club, and formed the Houston Ladies Golf Association. Frankie Randolph pursued golf just as she would later pursue politics—playing to win. She participated in tournaments and once became a runner-up in a state women's golf competition.

Horses were another of her passions. Deke Randolph shared his wife's enthusiasm for horseback riding, playing polo at the Houston Riding and Polo Club on Westheimer. Marguerite Johnston recalled the Randolphs as a "handsome couple" on horseback, and that Deke "rode his gaited horses with the grace and ease of an aristocrat." He and Frankie hired architect John Staub to build a stable for their horses on South Post Oak Lane, and the couple laid out bridle trails and jumps.

Other Houston couples built houses in the "country" and rode from house to house on horseback. So prevalent was the love of riding, polo, swimming, and tennis among Houstonians that Deke Randolph was one of a group that formed the Bayou Club in 1938. There the Randolphs, with their daughters Aubrey, born May 28, 1919, and Jean, born November 19, 1922, could indulge in sports to their hearts' content.

Frankie Randolph was always up for fun. Her nieces recall fun-filled weekends to Camden and their aunt taking flocks of girls to swim at Houston's Natatorium and then driving them around Glenwood Cemetery. Frankie kept horses at Camden, and there she leveled out an area at the foot of a hill to practice her golf swings. It was the job of nieces and nephews to keep her miniature practice range well weeded.

As Houston and Camden in the summertime were both hot and humid, the entire Carter clan often vacationed at Lake George, New York, at a lodge that Maude Holley Carter bought after W. T.'s death. Frankie spent every day at nearby Saratoga, encouraging her nieces to bet their allowances on horses racing at the Saratoga tracks. When her nieces lost, Frankie would reimburse them. "She was just so much fun and just so good!" her niece Mary Carroll Reed remembered of those golden days.

Frankie was an avid horseracing enthusiast, following one horse, Sarazan, from Saratoga to Aquaduct to Belmont and making "a killing" on his wins. However, when she bet on another horse, which came in first but then was disqualified, she "quit the races."

THREE

Going Forward

*I*n the period before the outbreak of World War II, Frankie Randolph's life seemed to be complete. As dedicated sportswoman, mother of two young children, and devoted member of the Junior League, she led a full and active life. Her league activities, however, opened the door to community for her and led her to enter the world of business.

In June 1929 the Houston Junior League obtained their first building through Joseph S. Cullinan's gift of land just outside the gates of Courtlandt Place. The league hired John Staub to design a building for them and planned large rooms on the second floor for meetings, lectures, and musicales (later they would often rent the space for high-school dances). The Luncheon Club moved to the new location on Stuart Avenue and continued its success.

The ground floor was designed for shops intended to generate more income for the league. Randolph formed a partnership with Georgina Williams to open the Patio Shop, a millinery and dressmaking establishment. With the nation on the brink of the Great Depression, it was hardly a propitious time for two women to begin a business venture, but friends and fellow league members patronized the establishment.

When Williams's African-American chauffeur contracted syphilis, the two women were outraged when Jeff Davis Hospital would not admit him for treatment. They mounted a campaign that forced the hospital to admit the man. This was Randolph's first glimpse into the world of discrimination against African Americans. She and Williams began going to city council meetings, became involved in city charter revision, and began to take an active part in Houston politics, with Randolph becoming an active member of the League of Women Voters and serving as finance chairman of the group. During this period, Randolph was also instrumental in putting together the Wednesday Club, an informal group that brought together people of a variety of interests to discuss issues of importance on both the national and local levels. Her commitment to community service continued also. She served as a volunteer for the Community Chest in its Social Service Bureau, taking eight families and reporting on their needs to the organization.

In 1940 she was a founder of the Citizens Charter Committee, working avidly, along with Will Clayton and his wife, Susan, a former suffragist and then the state Democratic committeewoman, to bring the city manager form of government to Houston. In 1938 amendments to the city charter were proposed to inaugurate the city manager form instead of the mayor-council form that was traditional in Houston, but the amendments were defeated by some 400 votes.

The League of Women Voters advocated and worked for a change in the charter in 1942. Dissatisfied with health conditions and health services to the community, the league trumpeted its campaign slogan, "Better Health through Better Government" across the city, opened a headquarters, and fervently worked for changes. Frankie Randolph was in the forefront of the campaign, in charge of precinct organization—a task that she would master in her work with Democratic politics.

On August 15, 1942, joining Cincinnati and Kansas City, Houston became the third large metropolitan city in the United States to inaugurate the city manager form of government, and Randolph embarked on her career as a political campaigner and organizer. Houston's love affair with the city manager form of government was short-lived, however, and by 1946, the mayor-council form of government was reinstated. In the 1947 election, Houston's "Old Gray Mayor," Oscar B. Holcombe, was back in office.

In 1950 Randolph once again united with Clayton and his wife, plus organized labor, to fight for public housing in Houston, an issue that was opposed by private housing interests and defeated in a referendum sent to the Houston voters.

Later in her life, Randolph said that "Liberalism to me means going forward instead of living in the past." By the 1940s, Texas was decidedly living in the past, and conservative forces were at work that threatened both liberal thought and action throughout the state. Randolph's firm sense of social justice and her strong support of "people issues" ranked her as a liberal in a state that was increasingly turning conservative. Fighting against conservative forces in Texas propelled Randolph into the Texas political arena. In true Frankie fashion, she never looked back.

The stage was set for women to enter into politics in the 1940s, when the warhorse of Texas women's activism, Minnie Fisher Cunningham, threw her hat into the gubernatorial ring in 1944 as a challenge to incumbent Texas governor Coke Stevenson, who was running for reelection. Cunningham, one of the members of the "Petticoat Lobby," who had spearheaded the fight for women's suffrage, was one of the leaders of the Democratic party that Randolph would work with and learn from.

Cunningham was also one of the two hundred women who met in the Texas House of Representatives on September 7, 1944, to discuss ways of increasing participation in the state's politics. "Minnie Fish" spoke out in support of women taking a more active role in state government and politics. Her rousing speech might well have sounded as a clarion call to Randolph, for as Bernard Rapoport recalled, " 'Minnie Fish' could turn on a crowd like no one I've ever known."

Liberal forces in Texas had hoped to persuade University of Texas professor J. Frank Dobie, an outspoken defender of liberal causes, to run against Stevenson, but when he refused, Cunningham entered the race. Although she lost to Stevenson,

Cunningham and the liberals forced the governor to stay in Texas campaigning to keep his office and kept Stevenson from leading the state's delegation to the Democratic National Convention. For the first time in the history of Texas politics, the governor did not control the so-called governor's convention in September.

While the liberals had managed to hamstring the governor on the national scene, the Texas Regulars, composed of the extreme right-wing conservatives within the Democratic party, continued their fight in opposition to President Franklin Roosevelt's reelection. Anti-New Deal, anti-Roosevelt, anti-Henry Wallace, and anti-labor, the Texas Regulars would soon be in the forefront of firing Dr. Homer P. Rainey as president of the University of Texas. The firing of Rainey and liberal university professors of economics, combined with the university regents' banning from the curriculum books they considered "obscene," mobilized the state's liberals in a fight for academic freedom that brought Texas national headlines.

One of the groups formed to protest the firings at the university was the Women's Committee on Educational Freedom, organized in January 1945. Members included former suffragists Jane McCallum and "Minnie Fish." The actions of the Women's Committee, combined with the protests of other liberal groups, led the American Association of University Professors and the Southern Association of Colleges and Secondary Schools to place the university on probation.

The year 1946 was an important one for Texas liberals. Homer P. Rainey announced that he would challenge four conservative candidates for governor. Swelled by membership after World War II, the Congress of Industrial Organizations was also on its way to organizing successfully in Texas. Opposition to the CIO mounted within conservative business interests, directed toward the labor group's organizing of African Americans, their support of the Fair Employment Practices Committee, and their efforts to abolish the poll tax.

In addition, in February 1946, Heman Sweatt, an African-American postal worker from Houston, backed by the NAACP, began his four-year fight to enter the law school at the University of Texas. In the landmark decision *Sweatt v. Painter*, the Supreme Court in 1950 agreed with the plaintiffs that the creation of an all-black law school would inherently offer an inferior education in comparison with the university and ordered the university to open its doors to Sweatt. The desegregation of the undergraduate school soon followed. Each of these issues would have a profound effect on Democratic politics across the state and on Frankie Randolph's political commitment.

The pivotal 1948 election saw Texas split along liberal-conservative lines, with Frankie Randolph firmly in the liberal camp. When Congressman Lyndon Johnson, smarting from his defeat for a U.S. Senate seat in the 1941 election, announced he would run for the Senate in 1948, he was challenged by former Texas governor "Calculating Coke" Stevenson. Like most Texas liberals, Randolph backed Johnson, beginning an uneasy alliance that would be torn apart in 1956.

While organized labor stood in opposition to Johnson on the grounds of his vote for the Taft-Hartley bill and his vote to override Truman's veto of the bill that allowed states to set up "right-to-work" laws, the CIO made no endorsement in the race but secretly helped Johnson. In addition, Stevenson, as governor, had been more open to union demands than other conservative Texas executives. The American Federation of Labor (AFL) and the railroad brotherhoods endorsed Stevenson because of his opposition to Taft-Hartley.

When Texas governor Beauford Jester announced that he was opposed to the nomination of President Harry Truman, the labor-loyalists began organizing to see that Democrats in the state would remain loyal to the party's candidates. They would have a tough fight, and that fight would position Frankie Randolph in the forefront of those purging the party of Democrats who consistently voted Republican in national elections.

Another issue splitting the state into conservative and liberal camps was one that became known as the "tidelands." Using their states rights' stance, conservatives in Texas were claiming all revenues from oil discovered in submerged lands off the Texas Gulf Coast. In 1947 the United States Supreme Court had ruled that California did not own its tidelands, setting a precedent for national control of the state's oil rich tidelands. The Texas Regulars and conservative Texans stood firmly on the side of the state's claims to its tidelands, an issue that would be of major importance in the politics of the 1950s.

With conservatives abandoning Truman, fighting against the CIO's organizing tactics in Texas, taking an anti-civil rights stand, and adhering closely to state control of the tidelands, labor-loyalists, in May 1948, calling for party loyalty from all Democrats and support for President Truman, went down in defeat at the state Democratic convention in Brownsville. They bolted the convention and held a rump session in a converted mule or cowbarn. Many of the liberal-loyalists proudly claimed their new identification as "cowbarn Democrats."

Although Governor Jester called for a slate of uninstructed delegates to the national convention, labor-loyalists won a significant victory when Truman soundly defeated Republican Tomas Dewey in the state. However, when Governor Jester died in office in July 1949, Lieutenant Governor Allan Shivers, a charismatic leader who supported state ownership of the tidelands and a decided foe of labor, came to the governor's office. In Shivers, the labor-loyalists would meet their staunchest foe. Despite the fact that he would take a pledge of strict party loyalty in 1950, by 1951 the governor signed into law a bill allowing candidates of one Texas political party to cross-file as candidates of another political party.

The actions of Shivers set the stage for a hardcore fight between conservatives and the labor-loyalists that would dominate Texas politics for years to come. Liberals and labor perceived the governor's actions as an attempt to lead the state into the Republican column in 1952, and, combined with Shivers's efforts to purge the State Democratic Executive Committee of liberal members, duly elected from their districts, put the labor-loyalists and Shivers on a collision course.

Shivers continued to straddle the fence, speaking out against Truman, while not actively asking Texans to vote Republican. His own political position remained in jeopardy at this juncture, as Austin attorney Fagan Dickson wrote to Walter G. Hall: "If he [Shivers] ever once says that he will not support the nominee of the Democratic party, he is gone politically. On the other hand, if he says that he will support the nominee of the Democratic party, even if it is Truman, the Dixiecrats will quit him and the Republicans will think he has reversed himself."

Liberals consolidated their efforts into an *ad hoc* group called the Loyal Democrats of Texas, calling for all delegates to the national convention to sign a loyalty pledge to support the Democratic party and its candidates. They also called for amending the Taft-Hartley bill and called for a civil-rights plank in the national Democratic platform.

Despite the fact that Sam Rayburn had announced his support of the Loyal Democrats of Texas, he basically did little to see that their causes were advanced. Shivers convinced Rayburn that he would support the Democratic party, but then began speaking out against President Truman and his policies, plus advancing scathing attacks against the Supreme Court and its tidelands decision.

The battle lines were drawn at the Democratic state convention in May 1952. When the loyalists called for a loyalty oath in support of the Democratic national ticket, the Shivers forces booed. With former New Deal congressman Maury Maverick, Sr., sounding the rallying cry, "Who will go with me to La Villita?," the loyalist delegates, led by Maverick and Fagan Dickson, bolted and marched in the rain to San Antonio's historic district. Years later, Ralph Yarborough remembered the walkout at La Villita and a priest giving an invocation: "Lord, help them; they have so far to go."

Basically, by this time, Texas had two Democratic parties, and which one would be seated at the national convention was the question. But even before the San Antonio loyalist group could leave for the convention, controversy arose over the make-up of the delegation.

Fagan Dickson was to lead the loyalist delegation to the convention, and Kathleen Voight had been chosen as a delegate. However, San Antonio attorney Herschel Bernard came to Voight and told her that there were over one hundred delegates going, and not one was Hispanic. Bernard asked her to give up her place in order that Albert Pena could be part of the delegation, and Voight agreed. Bernard also convinced Bernard Lifshutz to give up his place so that G. J. Sutton could represent San Antonio's African-American population.

With the national convention set for Chicago in July, Major Jubal R. Parten and Maverick were to head the Texas loyalists as they challenged the so-called Shivercrats. Voight later said that Maverick called on Harry Truman and that the president promised to help seat the loyalists. During hearings before the credentials committee, with a brief signed by Creekmore Fath, Fagan Dickson, and Austin attorney John D. Cofer (a brief argued by Cofer), loyalists proudly displayed their "Seat Texas Mavericks" sign and offered to go home if the Shivercrats would sign a loyalty oath to support the party's candidates.

The "Maverick" protests were to no avail, as the Shivercrats were seated as the delegates from Texas, after agreeing that the nominees of the Democratic convention would be on the Texas ballot. In September 1952 the Texas Democratic party met in convention in Amarillo. Although Shivers had promised Rayburn that he would support the party's candidates, he denounced Adlai Stevenson, the party's nominee for the presidency, for his stand on the tidelands issue, and turned his back on the party to support Republican Dwight D. Eisenhower.

Voight and other delegates were "horrified," and Rayburn, furious with Shivers over the broken promise, never spoke to the governor again. Rayburn told Voight and others, "I don't even want that fellow coming to my funeral."

FOUR

Fighting for Adlai and Ralph

Democratic political activist Eddie Ball remembered the day in 1952 when Frankie Randolph and a friend walked into Stevenson-Sparkman campaign headquarters in Houston and volunteered. Randolph handed him a check for a thousand dollars and announced, "I'm Frankie Randolph. What can I do to help?"

Grateful for the monetary contribution, Ball was even more grateful for the offer of time. He needed someone to spearhead an organization to compile a list of all the liberal-loyal Democrats in Harris County from the records of the 1948 and 1950 elections. He explained his long-term goal to Randolph—to put together a "permanent organization of the liberal-loyal Democrats outside the party structure." Such an organization had long been on Ball's mind, along with those of other liberals in Texas.

Sam Rayburn, still the political leader of the Democratic party in Texas, was opposed to any group that worked outside the party structure, and he and Ball had locked horns over the issue. "We fussed and feuded with him ... from the word go," Ball said. Ball had taken a leave of absence from working in labor lawyer Chris Dixie's office to head the Truman-Barkley campaign headquarters for the 1948 race, but he had been fired for trying to form a permanent organization outside the party.

Nevertheless, he was convinced a permanent organization was needed, and Randolph caught his enthusiasm. According to Ball, "I set her up with a couple of rooms in the headquarters with typewriters. We got volunteers. She put together a list of loyal Democrats. . . . It was this list we used to invite people to meetings during the following year and formed the Harris County Democrats."

The Harris County organization proved to be a most effective organizational arm of a later statewide group, the Democrats of Texas. Randolph was the organizational impetus, keeping all the records and seeing that the clerical work was done. Ball recalled that Randolph "rose through sheer hard work. She would come in every day and stay all day. She became close friends with everyone who was a leader in Harris County and eventually statewide."

Melding the various liberal elements in the county into a harmonious group was difficult, as when the group was formed, Anglo liberals were making all the decisions. African Americans and labor were supposed to turn out votes. Ball and other organizers were determined that labor and African Americans would have equal voices in decision making. Bringing these groups into the decision-making process took time and effort; in the past many of the rank-and-file within the labor movement, particularly the CIO, were opposed to civil rights.

Throughout the South, the building trades had set up what were known as "Jim Crow" locals, where Anglos and African Americans were separated. Ball remembered that about five plants in the Houston area had Jim Crow locals among the steelworkers, but through meetings and discussions, the locals gradually came together. He said that by 1952 "the leadership of the CIO had pretty much accepted the fact that civil rights was an issue that would not go away."

Furthermore, the Harris County Democrats determined that all three facets of the group would have the right to caucus and to exercise a veto against any endorsement made by the group. No endorsement would be made unless all three facets agreed. This was the first time that African Americans could exercise their right to be part of the endorsement process.

For Frankie Randolph, the bringing together of the three facets of the group presented a crisis of conscience. She also had to make a decision, and a pivotal one— whether to side with the Anglo establishment within the liberal wing or with labor and the African Americans. She talked at length with Ball and went with labor and the African Americans.

The Harris County Democrats became the training ground where Randolph put her organizational skills to work for the building of the labor-liberal wing of the Democratic party in Texas. Working within the structure of the organization, Eddie Ball began putting together schools to teach loyal Democrats the basics of precinct organization, the rules and regulations of voting, and the groundwork of party politics. It was up to Randolph to conduct the schools, train workers to become floor leaders at the county and state conventions, and to help maintain the liberal presence within the Democratic party. She gained the admiration of Ball. "As an organizer, Frankie Randolph was supreme," he said. "She was able to identify people who would work and she could motivate them to work."

In addition to trying to elect Adlai Stevenson on the national scene, Texas liberals had another political challenge closer to home. East Texan Ralph Yarborough had announced for the governor's office against Allan Shivers, and the race proved to be a classic liberal-conservative fight. Like Speaker Sam Rayburn and many liberals across Texas, Randolph was an ardent supporter of Yarborough.

Although Shivers won reelection to the governor's office by more than a million votes, Ralph Yarborough gained valuable political experience from the race, much of it from Randolph. The Harris County Democrats came out full force for Yarborough, seeing him as a viable liberal challenge to the conservatism of Shivers. Prior to the 1952 governor's race, Yarborough's political base had been primarily East Texas, and with the statewide race, he gained practical political experience that would serve him well in other political races, both for the governor's office and for the United States Senate.

Ball recalled that Yarborough held a personal grudge against Shivers over some presumed slight, and at first, the candidate had a difficult time positioning himself against the conservative governor. Ball remembered:

> He didn't come on the scene as a raving liberal. In fact he was kind of embarrassed at having our [the Harris County Democrats'] support. But we worked for him, getting out the crowds when he spoke and arranging meetings for him.
>
> Frankie Randolph raised a lot of money for Ralph. And he learned a lot about policy from her. He knew very little about issues such as workers' compensation or civil rights. He became informed on issues partially through conversations with her.... Ralph had great admiration for her, ... and he trusted her more than he trusted labor leaders. He ran a much better race in 1954, and much of it was because of her.

Randolph was indefatigable in reaching out and making contact with anyone who would work for loyal Democratic candidates, often recruiting liberals to the cause. One of her precinct organizers, Bud Mosier, recalled that the two would often attend two meetings in one night, but by nine the next morning, Randolph was back at her desk, hard at work. Mosier said of her: "She was the most remarkable person I ever met in my life, and after I found out she really meant business, that she wasn't just 'whistling Dixie,' I just got totally committed."

With Stevenson and Yarborough both going down in defeat in 1952, and with Shivers firmly in control of the Democratic party in Texas, loyalists intensified their efforts to establish a permanent organization outside the party. With Stevenson's defeat to Eisenhower and with Governor Allan Shivers and his "Shivercrats" in control of the state's political apparatus, in May 1953 a group of labor-loyalists, including Randolph, met at Buchanan Dam outside of Austin to begin rebuilding the liberal wing of the party.

The organization they established was called the Texas Democratic Organizing Committee, commonly known as the DOC, designed to organize statewide loyalist groups, to select Democratic committeemen and women from each senatorial district in tune with the labor-loyalists' views, and to publish a "pamphlet" that would help return the Texas Democratic party to loyalist Democrats. Byron Skelton, a lawyer from Temple, was chosen chairperson of the group, with Lillian Collier as vice-chair, and Creekmore Fath as secretary-treasurer.

Although the group was successful, the national Democratic party took a dim view of any group functioning outside party ranks. When Stephen Mitchell, chair of the national Democratic party, arrived in Texas in June 1953, he told the DOC in no uncertain terms that the national party was setting up a Democratic Advisory Council to be known as the DAC, and, according to Fath, they had to "scuttle the DOC to make the DAC a success."

Eddie Ball had several hundred dollars left over from the Stevenson campaign, and although he wanted to use the funds to set up a permanent organization, Speaker Rayburn insisted that the funds be sent to him. Ball and others finally agreed, with the stipulation that the funds be reserved for Texans who were working for the loyalist Democrats. According to Ball, "When we went to get the money, there wasn't any. Rayburn had used the money for distributions to Congressmen for their races. He needed their support during his campaign for speaker, and he didn't want an organization he couldn't control."

On December 13, 1953, at a meeting of the DOC executive committee, dissension among the loyalists was evident. A majority of the group voted to dissolve the DOC when the DAC was established. Delegates from Harris, Denton, and Bee counties objected, and the most vocal opposition came from Creekmore Fath. When the DAC was formed, Rayburn put out the word that Fath was not to be a DAC member from Austin, and Frankie Randolph recalled that the "liberal loyalists on the DAC put pressure on Rayburn to accept Fath's appointment." Tensions between the loyalists and the DAC would continue to grow.

Meanwhile, the loyalists took up the banner for Yarborough, who, in 1954, once again challenged Allan Shivers for the governor's office. Before the primary, loyalists went to work, spread-

ing the news that this time Yarborough might well win and solid-
ifying his name identification across the state.

The Texas Democratic Women's State Committee was in the
forefront of the campaign, with Minnie Fisher Cunningham,
Lillian Collier, Frankie Randolph, and other Democratic women
commanding local precinct organizations and targeting voters
with mailouts and telephones.

In addition, while many of Texas's wealthy stood solidly behind Governor Shivers, Randolph, Jubal R. Parten, Will Clayton, and others contributed $3,000 each to Yarborough. Organ-
ized labor's political action money also helped mightily with the
Yarborough effort to unseat Shivers, who was trying for a third
term as the state's governor.

Shivers, who enjoyed a scandal-free administration, for his
first two terms, was plagued with insurance scandals and rumors
about fraudulent business deals concerning his real estate holdings in the Rio Grande Valley. Campaigning around the state,
Yarborough made inroads into the governor's moderate supporters, but Shivers struck back.

Honing in on the mounting "red scare" and fear of communist infiltration into union activities in Texas, Shivers linked
a CIO strike in Port Arthur directly to communists. He went further by appointing an industrial commission to investigate the
role of communists in Texas union activities. The commission,
dominated by conservative businessmen, found that communist-
dominated unions would indeed be moving into Texas and rec-
ommended that laws be passed outlawing the communist party.

Even more hurtful to Yarborough's campaign for governor
was the race issue. In the wake of the U.S. Supreme Court's
groundbreaking decision in *Brown vs. Board of Education of To-
peka, Kansas*, Texas, like other states, was mandated to integrate
its public schools with all deliberate speed. Shivers, who announced that the decision was "an unwarranted invasion of the
constitutional rights of the states," ordered Texas schools not to
integrate and challenged Yarborough on his stand concerning
segregation.

Knowing that the majority of Texans favored segregation,
Yarborough tried to avoid the issue, but spoke out in favor of

separate but "genuinely equal" schools, refusing to attack the Supreme Court decision or to support segregation. His moderate stance lost him not only many white conservative votes, but also votes among African Americans and labor who felt he should have spoken out in favor of the Court's decision.

Nevertheless, when the votes were counted in the primary, Yarborough had come within 23,000 votes of the incumbent governor. Shivers's campaign and public relations teams poured on the heat, circulating photographs of Anglo women and African-American men walking a picket line together, photographs that union leaders claimed were faked. Their main campaign weapon was a film, "The Port Arthur Story," depicting the coastal town, the keystone of the Gulf Coast petrochemical complex and the governor's hometown, as a "ghost town," with plants idle and an economy at the breaking point. Laying the death of the town's industry at the feet of communist-inspired union workers who supported Yarborough, the film was widely circulated. Few knew that the film had been photographed early in the morning, before plants were opened or workers had begun their shifts.

Businessmen were bombarded with material alleging that if Yarborough were elected, Texas would be unionized, while the Shivers camp put out photographs that had been retouched to make Yarborough appear to be of African-American ancestry. On the campaign trail in South Texas, Yarborough would be greeted by exploding devices, burning crosses, and virulent newspaper articles.

Bolstered by fraudulent campaign tactics, Shivers swept to victory, but Yarborough had lost by only 122,000 votes—a sizable gain over his totals in 1952. Liberal-loyalists were convinced that they had their candidate, one who would carry their issues and policies to the statehouse. However, with Shivers dominating the votes in major cities across the state, and winning the endorsements of the major newspapers, liberals knew they needed a vehicle that would challenge the conservative press and bring their issues to the attention of Texas voters.

FIVE

Founding
the Texas Observer

Looking for a journalistic vehicle which would provide a venue for liberal candidates and issues to be brought to the attention of Texans across the state, Minnie Fisher Cunningham and Lillian Collier began searching for a newspaper. In 1953, Franklin Jones, Sr., and other "amateur journalists" began publishing the *East Texas Democrat*, while the *State Observer* had proved to be an outstanding independent voice for liberal views and issues.

Cunningham and Collier traveled to Marshall, Texas, where the *East Texas Democrat* was published, visited with Jones, and determined to make the *Democrat* a statewide newspaper. Jones later recalled that the group visited a number of wealthy Democrats in the city to request funding for the venture, and left empty-handed. He said, "I agreed to ask our board to give, devise and bequeath to them the *East Texas Democrat* with all its shortcomings, and to help them arrange for someone else to take it over. Little did any of us envision the *Texas Observer*."

A group of liberal backers met at the Driskill Hotel in Austin to choose an editor for the journal and to discuss the editorial policies to be followed. Jones was among the group and remembered that Jimmy Strong told him his brother Jack had suggested Ronnie Dugger, who had been the feisty and hard-hitting editor of the *Daily Texan* during his college days at the University of Texas.

Dugger was on his way to Mexico to do some freelance writing, but met with Jones and others. At first he refused, feeling that he wanted no part of a ". . . hack political organ, no part of a journalism controlled by a politically motivated board of directors. If they would let me have exclusive control of the editorial contents . . . I would do it."

Jones sent in Dugger's conditions to the group, and Mark Adams, also under consideration as editor of the *Observer*, noted that, "If ever a rattlesnake rattled before it struck, Dugger did."

Some liberals had qualms about even beginning the venture, and Bob Eckhardt, then a labor lobbyist for the CIO, expressed his, stating that lack of funding had defeated the crusading *Texas Spectator*, a weekly edited by Hart Stillwell and Herbert Mewhinney. Eckhardt felt that the funding needed to publish the *Observer* would draw campaign contributions from liberal candidates.

Dugger returned that afternoon to again discuss the editorship with the group. When he approached the double doors of the meeting room, he yielded to a woman "who was introduced to me as Mrs. R. D. Randolph." The meeting would prove a historic one for both Dugger and Randolph.

The group accepted Dugger's conditions, and he accepted their offer of the editorship. Jones felt that "It was not so much our persuasion, I believe, as the challenge of becoming an editor that interested Ronnie Dugger. I sent in his famous list of conditions. . . . Ronnie made his customary captivating appeal, and for better or worse, the *Texas Observer* was launched."

Political activist Billie Carr remembered that Randolph was instrumental in choosing Dugger for the position and that she was determined that the editor be young, intellectual, and full of integrity. To Randolph, Dugger met all those qualifications. "She was the best at picking people there was," Carr said, "and she knew that Ronnie was 'it'."

Dugger himself stated his views clearly and succinctly in a

letter to Randolph that was published in one of the final editions of the *State Observer*. He wrote: "Let me say candidly, that I would not want to try to edit the present *Observer* 'bare,' as it were—trying to carry on without a change of format, adequate staff, and a promotional campaign." He also stated his ideas concerning "independent journalism" in a letter to Franklin Jones: "We need a newspaper that will report all the facts the people have a right to know without fear of any individual, group, or public prejudice—a free newspaper, financed by enlightened independents, as individuals, so that its editorial staff may pursue the traditions of honest and aggressive journalism."

For a time, the newspaper was run by a committee, the group having melded the *East Texas Democrat* and the *State Observer*. Randolph loaned the corporation, the Texas Observer Publishing Company, $5,000; an additional $5,000 was sold in stock. Before the name was even settled on, liberal-loyalists wrote out blank checks for stock in the publication.

With Randolph serving as treasurer of the corporation and as one of the trustees, the *Observer* began. However, rule by committee was often difficult. Jones remembered "the horrors of the transition period between operation by a committee and the day Mrs. R. D. Randolph became publisher in name as well as in fact."

As treasurer, Randolph kept scrupulous records, submitting monthly reports on expenses to the accountants until the 1960s. She made meticulous handwritten notes on the expenses of the journal before submitting the typewritten accounts. On December 16, 1957, the accountant R. H. Bentley wrote to Randolph concerning amounts she had contributed to the journal. He suggested that for tax purposes she list these funds as notes payable to her since she would be able "to claim the loss for tax purposes as a loss from the partnership."

While some might have felt that Randolph, having loaned a sizable amount to the corporation, would insist on playing a primary role, she gave Dugger a free hand. She served as publisher, he as editor, and she lived up to the group's decision, giving him absolute control of all editorial policy and over all material going into the publication. In an interview concerning the *Observer*'s initial years, Dugger commented: "Mrs. Randolph from the very beginning was totally devoted to the idea of independent journalism, of an independent journal, and of the editor running it."

Disagreements, however, did arise, both with Dugger and then with his successor, Willie Morris, but she never interfered with their running of the *Observer*. Nevertheless, Randolph was a formidable force. Dugger recalled that "Mrs. Randolph trusted me; and when we differed, and I was arguing to her that she was wrong, I can't tell you how carefully I would proceed."

By June 1960, Dugger felt that the journal was in trouble. In a confidential letter to Randolph and other financial backers of the *Observer*, he wrote that "the overhead has not been met by the income. We have not been able to break through with advertising. . . . The burden has become more than Mrs. Randolph can continue to sustain beyond the fall of 1960." Dugger explained he felt that he had said to the *Observer*'s readership "most of what I have to say about politics and certain areas of neglected reform," and suggested that he step down as editor but continue to contribute articles to the paper. He suggested as editor Willie Morris, who had also been an editor of the *Daily Texan*. Morris, as editor, would, according to Dugger, "bring new ideas, new styles, new subject matter, and new challenges to the liberal movement in Texas."

At that time a Rhodes Scholar in history at Oxford University, Morris had worked as associate editor of the *Observer* during a summer, and Dugger suggested that he once again be appointed associate editor and eventually take over the editorship. Morris took over the paper in 1961 and established the same working relationship with Randolph. She told him, "This is a free paper. You're the editor, and the paper is yours."

Morris, who wrote of Randolph as "the Eleanor Roosevelt of Texas," recalled that when the paper inevitably was in financial straits, she would come to its aid with another sizable check, explaining, "Some old ladies collect antiques. . . . I want to make the place we live in better." Randolph spoke from experience, as, in the years before she entered politics, she had collected antiques—so many that she had to rent a warehouse to store them all. Creekmore Fath, who had participated in all the political battles of the 1950s with Randolph, remembered being in Houston on one occasion and having drinks with both Frankie and Deke Randolph. Deke commented that he didn't know what he was going to do about Frankie, as she was "spending all the goddamn money on politics." Frankie looked at her husband and commented wryly, "Would you rather I go back to collecting antiques?"

Willie Morris summed up his admiration for her simply: "I loved Mrs. Randolph." He recalled that throughout the late 1950s and 1960s, she would often have groups of liberals meeting at her Houston home, discussing "the minimum wage, racial prejudice, the evils of the oil depletion allowance, and the John Birchers," all issues of importance to liberals and issues that found their way into the pages of the journal she had helped found.

The journal, "that obstreperous and mischievous child," according to Jones, has proven to be just what its backers, including Randolph, determined it would be, a true "journal of free voices," tackling progressive issues, exposing corruption, informing the public on issues concerning civil and human rights, and, most importantly, covering the peccadilloes of the Texas legislature.

The *Observer's* coverage of the "lege," by itself, would have rated it awards for both humor and investigative reporting, for as Morris wrote: "Until 1955, when the *Observer* writers were set loose on it, the Texas legislature had seldom expected to be taken seriously. It was a circus of ordinary follies, a lane-end; stagnating in the backwaters of provincial politics."

During the 1950s and 1960s, with writers such as Dugger, Morris, Robert Sherrill, and Larry Goodwyn covering committee meetings, interviewing both legislators and lobbyists, and turning their critical eye to the "goings on" of the legislature while in session and during interims, the *Observer* soon became a "must read" for anyone involved in the legislative process.

During its formative years, the *Observer* fulfilled its mission, often publishing stories and exposing issues that major newspapers across the state failed to cover. To Morris, that is what set the paper apart. In his memoir, *North Toward Home*, Morris recalled his first visit to the Texas Senate for a floor debate: "A young reporter turned to me and asked 'How can I tell the truth about what it's *really* like over here in a news story?' Under the format of a daily newspaper it is impossible. A good journalist with a mind of his own can see right through the deceits. He knows the man is lying and he knows the man knows he's lying. It is like a game. Indignant outbursts are accompanied by sly grins; laughter creeps into the most heartfelt speeches. Nothing whatever has the ring of truth."

During the 1970s the editorship of the *Observer* was shared by two women journalists, Kaye Northcott and Molly Ivins, a move that Frankie Randolph surely would have approved. As publisher, Dugger believed the two "delivered the *Observer* from the chauvinism that is an organic part of the Texas way," and noted that while "Kaye ran a tight ship," Molly "gave us laughter."

The editors managed the journal during its most expansive period, the period that reflected the Vietnam era and the Watergate scandal, a period that saw the *Observer*'s readership grow to 14,500 in 1972. Long hours and low pay continued to mark the publication, but the writing on the Texas legislature and issues pertinent to social justice continued to be read by politicians both in Texas and in Washington.

Ivins remembered that she was paid only $125 a week but still thought she had "the best job in American journalism, and money was never an issue: I loved working on the *Observer*, and I didn't mind one bit that it didn't pay much. What did I care? I was young. I was healthy. I didn't have a family. I met fabulous people."

Ivins spent six years as co-editor of the *Observer*, years she considered to be her maturing years in the world of journalism. "Some people think of their college years as the happy, golden time. Writing for the *Observer* was my golden time, a time of joy, laughter—and learning." Part of the learning was working with Dugger, Goodwyn, and Morris, and she noted that in her "graduate school": "You study under the moral suasion of Ronnie Dugger, who walks on a higher moral plane than most mortals on this earth. You have that fabulous journalistic tradition to live up to, and you get to make your own mistakes. That is, of course, the greatest privilege of all." Many of Ivins's *Observer* articles found their way into the three collections of essays she published, and her articles on the Texas legislature remain some of her most pungent and hilarious.

In the 1970s the *Observer* found yet another patron, one who would pick up the deficit in the advertising sector. Bernard Rapoport, supporter of many liberal causes and a future regent of the University of Texas, began taking full-page ads in the journal under the banner of his American Income Life Insurance Company, based in Waco. Instead of merely advertising his company, Rapoport used the page to write timely political essays.

Had Frankie Randolph made no other contribution to the political life of Texas, her founding and financial backing of the *Texas Observer* would have won her accolades among liberals and journalists alike. She would have relished the salty humor of Jim Hightower, who inherited the editorship of the *Observer* in 1976. She would have applauded each of the editors, down to Louis Dubose, the current editor, who have continued the tradition of "free journalism" and maintained the *Observer's* determination to "serve no party or group but hew hard to the truth as we find it and the right as we see it."

On May 20, 1989, the *Observer* celebrated thirty-five years of publishing history with a benefit dinner at Palmer Auditorium in Austin. It was a joyous occasion, with politicians, journalists, and political activists paying $35 a plate to help defer the *Observer's* $35,000 debt. Dugger described the occasion as a "reuniting and reviving of the great Texas progressive coalition." Frankie Randolph would have applauded.

U.S. Senator Edward M. Kennedy gave the keynote speech at the dinner, and the honoree was former U.S. Senator Ralph Yarborough, who was given the Frankie Randolph Social Justice Award. Randolph, the driving force behind Yarborough's election to the Senate, would have loved it.

SIX

"Know who you've got and who you're gonna get"

*I*nspired by Ralph Yarborough's strong showing in the 1954 governor's race and by increasing press revelations of scandals in the governor's office, Frankie Randolph and other loyalist Democrats continued their organizational efforts. Their goal was to elect Yarborough governor of Texas in 1956 and solidify the loyalist Democratic opposition to the growing Republican presence in Texas which Shivers represented.

With their eyes firmly set on the 1956 governor's race, Frankie Randolph and the members of the Harris County Democrats set about organizing precinct by precinct. According to Chris Dixie, from its inception the organization of the Harris County Democrats was a fluid one: "Anybody who wanted to come in could come in. The ground rules were that nobody had to sell his soul to be a member for a day or for a year. He or she could be a member for any length of time, or could retire for a while and come in later."

As Randolph was the only member of the group with significant funds, she "soon occupied an unofficial position of absolute power. Whatever Frankie said was agreeable to one and all." As Randolph went to more and more organizational meetings among the members of the coalition, Eddie Ball would send back reports to Dixie concerning Randolph's participation in the group's activities. One report concerned the reactions of the head of the steelworkers' union. He responded to Randolph's gruff voice, saying, "I like her; she talks like a man."

However, talk was not all she did. She was a "fast learner," and became a staunch believer in precinct organization. She didn't think in terms of "this task is impossible." She determined that a precinct meeting was needed, scheduled it for a certain time, and rounded up the Democrats. On weekends she had Ralph Yarborough come to Houston and attend as many precinct meetings as possible to shore up his position after his 1954 loss. She got the word out: "Ralph's going to be there; he's coming to talk to you!"

Her formula for organizing precincts was to elect a secretary to be in charge and to write down names. Her motto was: "You've got to know who you've got and who you're gonna get." Then her job was to get information and help from Harris County Democrats headquarters to the precinct organizations.

So strong was her presence, so sure her plan for shoring up precinct strength, that no one seems to have thought it incongruous that here was a Houston society matron showing up to organize precincts in an expensive car driven by an African-American driver. She simply "got in the backseat of the car with her uniformed driver up front, and off she went to the Fifth Ward."

In addition, Randolph never seemed to use her money as muscle. Creekmore Fath remembered that "Frankie was wonderful . . . very easy to work with," while Eddie Ball recalled that "Frankie had great intellect. She would study the issues and become knowledgable about them. She and Ralph held many discussions between themselves and among other members of the Harris County Democrats. All their talk was on issues that affected labor-liberal politics."

One mark of Frankie Randolph's growing political strength was her election as vice-chair of the Democratic Advisory Council in March 1955. Liberal-loyalists had mixed feelings concerning the group, as it had been formed as Rayburn's answer to their formation of the Texas Democratic Organizing Committee.

Liberal-loyalists correctly saw that the DAC was essentially a move by Rayburn and Johnson to keep control of the Democratic party in Texas.

The prime function of the Democratic Advisory Council was to raise funds for the national committee to use for presidential and congressional races—functions that the State Democratic Executive Committee was expected to perform. However, with Shivers's appointees to the state committee showing no willingness to work with the national party, the members of the Democratic Advisory Council had their work cut out for them.

At the organizational meeting in Waco, the group established a sixteen-member steering committee and scheduled U.S. Senator Estes Kefauver of Tennessee, then testing the waters for his presidential run in 1956, to speak at Democratic rallies in Houston and San Antonio. Joining Randolph on the steering committee were Judge Jim Sewell as chairman, Byron Skelton, Kathleen Voight, Lillian Collier, and Truett Wylie.

Fath recalled that the DAC was an immediate success with its organizational plan. The committee divided the state into ten regions, and Voight was designated as organizing director. However, according to Fath, neither Rayburn nor Johnson were happy with the group's efforts, mainly because neither of them could control it.

When Estes Kefauver spoke in Houston on May 7, 1955, he was greeted by a tremendous ovation from the Democratic faithful. In addition, as Dixie remembered, another heartfelt ovation went to Frankie Randolph, a mark of her growing political strength within the labor-loyalists, particularly the Harris County Democrats.

By the time of the 1956 Democratic convention in Dallas, Frankie Randolph's political base was secure. According to Ball, "She was completely dedicated to creating and maintaining a Democratic organization in Harris County and here in Texas. She never wavered in her objectives."

In addition, Randolph's interest in social justice, and particularly in civil rights, was growing. She continued her reading on national issues, as well as issues in Texas. She also invited members of a variety of groups to her home to discuss the issues of the day. Beginning with the Wednesday Club, an interracial group that met informally to discuss social issues, she invited an eclectic mix of people from Houston socialites to labor leaders to discuss and debate topics or merely explore issues. The Wednesday Club began when a group of associates brought sandwiches to the precinct office and sat around discussing the issues. Gradually, the group expanded, and Randolph opened her home to the members.

Texas Observer editor Ronnie Dugger looked on her as both a progressive and a radical, a radical well before her time. After her death he commented that "in Houston Mrs. Randolph led what may have been historically the most powerful progressive movement in Texas since the farmers' populism of the preceding century." And he added: "She was a very moral person . . . very moralistic . . . and she had a strong internal integrity. She was concerned about the poor and she was concerned about the poor abroad as well as at home. She was a radical before it became fashionable to become a radical in this country."

During a time when Houston was a totally segregated Southern city, Randolph saw that civil rights was inevitable and expanded her working relations to include African Americans. One colleague, Gould Beech, a political organizer whose wife, Mary, served as Randolph's secretary-aide, said that "it always pained her to see black delegates to county conventions shunted off to the rear of the balcony," and when she was assigned to organize her first political banquet, she demanded that Houston's Shamrock Hotel allow African-American members of the organization to join the group for dinner. The Shamrock became one of the first hotels in Houston to integrate its restaurant facilities.

Randolph was not the only Houstonian who knew that civil rights were overdue for the city. Creekmore Fath pointed out that Jesse Jones, Houston's most acclaimed city father and owner of the Rice Hotel, allowed the owner of a black taxi company in Houston to park in the hotel's garage and to eat in the coffee shop. His admiration for the African-American business owner was heartfelt when he said of him: "He's as unique as Frankie Randolph!"

Others among Houston's establishment found her an oddity,

a wealthy woman who sided with labor against the prevalent conservative views of most Texans. Still, life for her was not all politics. She and Deke continued to ride horses, socialize, and raise their daughters amid Houston socialites.

Frankie enjoyed traveling, often to Lake George, New York, where her mother had enjoyed a respite from Houston's heat and humidity. Train travel had always seemed a great adventure to her since the days when W. T. Carter had simply hooked his private railroad car onto any train leaving East Texas, paying one fare for the entire family. Her ultimate getaway, however, continued to be Camden, deep in the East Texas pineywoods, where she, her sisters, and brothers built homes, and where she could escape the furors and foibles of Texas politics. Her daughters enjoyed the freedom of the rustic life in Camden, and when Aubrey married John Virgil Scott and Jean married David Longmaid, Frankie Randolph had grandchildren—Aubrey's Molly, Frances, and Jim, and Jean's Harry—to teach the lore and legends of the pineywoods. Nieces, nephews, grandnieces, and grandnephews all joined in the fun. Maude Lenoir Carter, her grandniece, remembered her aunt invariably wearing a denim skirt, white shirt, and red wedgies, playing solitaire, and overseeing or joining in their games.

With her gruff voice, though, Randolph could often be frightening to the children in the family and intimidating to others. Molly Luhrs, by all accounts a most favored grandchild, said that at Camden Randolph played a game with the grandchildren called "rip the flesh." "It was a great, fun game," recalled Luhrs. "Grandmother would turn off all the lights in the bedroom. My brother would be her helper, and I and my cousins would be the 'ripees.' We went into a frenzy trying to hide from her. She was not very tall, but she was fast. When she caught one of us, she would say, 'I'm going to rip your flesh.' Of course, she never did; but we weren't too sure." Deke warned her that she was frightening the children, but the game continued. No doubt, Randolph felt, like many of those times, that a little terror never hurt a child.

Luhrs said that her grandmother was very strict with the children at Camden. No child could go outside before breakfast.

They could swim only at ten in the morning and at five in the afternoon. They had to take naps from one to three in the afternoon. Woe be to the child who flaunted the rules, for Randolph kept two bullwhips—one in Camden and one in Houston. She always threatened to bullwhip them, and Luhrs remembered, "We believed her." She also would threaten them, by saying, "I'm going to cut your heads off and stick them on sticks."

As a child, Molly was both shy and sensitive, and her grandmother sensed that she was the one who needed the most attention. At mealtimes in Camden, Molly sat next to her grandmother at what was called "starvation corner." When the servants would pass the food, there was often very little left when they got to Molly.

Her grandmother always made Molly sit next to her and told her it was "so I can keep an eye on you," but in reality she did so probably just to be close to her. The children had to ask permission to go to the commissary or company store. Every morning before breakfast, Molly would ask to go, and her grandmother would sigh with exasperation and tell her: "Goddammit, Molly, if you ask me that one more time before breakfast, I'm not ever going to let you go."

Randolph had wanted her daughter Aubrey to follow in her footsteps, and it was a disappointment to her that neither of her daughters followed her into the political arena. Molly Luhrs became the chosen child, and Randolph passed down to her granddaughter her love of reading and of history. Luhrs followed her into an active political role, working with the Harris County Democrats, and even ran for precinct judge, but lost. She worked alongside Billie Carr, who inherited the mantle of Randolph's leadership of the Harris County Democrats, but Luhrs admitted, "I'll always work behind the scenes and help out. But I'm not my grandmother." Still, she said that it was "wonderful to have her as a mentor and role model. She was as tough as anyone I ever met on the outside . . ."

Her granddaughter summed up her admiration for Frankie Randolph: "I adored her with all my heart and soul."

SEVEN

Locking Horns
with Lyndon

By spring 1956 the battle lines in Texas were drawn. To check Governor Shivers's power in Texas and also to prevent loyalists from taking control of the party, Speaker Sam Rayburn threw Lyndon Johnson's hat into the presidential ring as a favorite-son candidate from Texas and the leader of the delegation to the Democratic National Convention. However, as events at the May convention proved, Rayburn and Johnson would find that walking a tightrope between the "Shivercrats" and the loyalists required major maneuvering on both their parts. As political organizer Kathleen Voight commented, the labor-loyalists "favored a weekend romance with Lyndon, but didn't want to marry him."

For the labor-loyalists, Lyndon Johnson's entry into the presidential race presented a dilemma. They knew they owed Rayburn their loyalty, for during a presidential election year, he invariably came to Texas and spent several months campaigning. And Rayburn was determined that Johnson would get the nomination.

The labor-loyalists decided they would support Johnson, but that they would control the delegates to the convention. They also determined that their choices for national committeeman and committeewoman would prevail. They spread the word across the state that Byron Skelton of Temple, one of the early organizers of the loyalist forces, was their choice for national committeeman. Their choice for national committeewoman was clearcut—Frankie Randolph.

Loyalists were firmly in control of many of the delegations going to the May 1956 Democratic convention in Dallas. The Bexar County delegation nominated Kathleen Voight for national committeewoman, but Voight indicated she would support Randolph. Several months before the convention, Randolph had telephoned Voight in San Antonio and asked her to fly to Houston to discuss the position of national committeewoman. According to Voight, Randolph's driver met her at the airport, and she "rode in splendor in the back seat of the car" to meet with Randolph.

The two political organizers had lunch at Randolph's home, and Randolph said to Voight: "I think we ought to make a deal. Both our names are up for national committeewoman. I think neither one of us ought to run. I think Lillian Collier should have it. She's been waiting for many years." Voight told Randolph that Collier was not wealthy enough, nor was she. "You have to be able to raise a whale of a lot of money," she later recalled. "But Frankie and I made a deal that we would be for Lillian Collier, but her name never came up."

When Voight arrived at the convention hall in Dallas, the move to elect Randolph was well under way. The Harris County Democrats had flooded the convention hall with flyers announcing her candidacy. "She had control of the *Texas Observer*, she had the money, and she had the influence," Voight said.

The Harris County delegation had done its work well, and by the time the convention opened, Randolph had the votes of the Harris, Tarrant, El Paso, Nueces, and Jefferson county delegations, with Bexar and Travis counties leaning in her favor. In addition, the Harris County Democrats, with Randolph in the forefront, urged delegates to purge the State Democratic Executive Committee of Governor Allan Shivers's supporters. On May 21, the day before the state convention, the Democratic Advisory Committee met in caucus, and Randolph addressed the group, urging them to to purge the committee of Shivers supporters.

Johnson knew he needed the support of the Shivers group and urged the DAC and the Harris County Democrats to back down. They adamantly refused. According to Eddie Ball, "Lyndon threw a fit. He felt we were not being sincere in our support for him . . . and he was right." The delegates remained adamant in their choices, and labor particulary insisted that Randolph be the committeewoman. "We were not going to let them destroy the organization, and we were going to have one of our spokespersons there—and that was Frankie Randolph," Ball remembered.

Johnson wanted only one member of the Democratic Advisory Committee in a national committee slot, and agreed to Byron Skelton, but he insisted on his choice for committeewoman—Beryl Ann Bentsen, wife of U.S. Congressman Lloyd Bentsen from the South Texas Valley. The choice was a slap in the face to labor, for B. A. Bentsen had not been active in Democratic political organization nor in any of the fights to hold the party in the Democratic column.

According to Ball, the loyalists told Lyndon he could name the committeeman, but they would name the committeewoman. The loyalists knew that Lyndon was already committed to Skelton and felt that they had the votes, particularly with the strength of the Harris County delegation, to elect Randolph. Johnson sent word to Randolph that he would see that other party positions were hers. In typical Frankie fashion, she answered with a resounding "No!"

Johnson refused to give in. He set up an office behind the stage at the convention, with John Connally in charge. Much of the pressure and arm twisting went on in that office. Ball later said that J. Edwin Smith, chair of the Harris County delegation, was to give the nominating speech for Randolph. Smith's greatest ambition was to be a United States judge, and Johnson called him back to the office, telling him, "J. Ed, if you pursue this, you'll never be a U.S. judge."

Ball recalled that Smith came out of the office, and the two men conferred. They talked about Johnson's edict, and then "J. Ed squared his shoulders, marched back in, and told Lyndon he would not back down."

Some did break ranks. Woodrow Bean from El Paso told Johnson he would support Bentsen, but the loyalists quickly got word back to his delegation to hold firm. Bean lost the vote, and then "had to go tell Lyndon he couldn't produce El Paso's vote."

The loyalists moved quickly to solidify Randolph's strength. They found a photograph of Beryl Ann Bentsen in the *Austin American-Statesman*, under the caption "Womanpower for Eisenhower." They printed up handbills with the photo and caption, with this disclaimer: "Do You Want This Republican to be your Democratic Chairwoman?" According to Ball, "This turned the tide. When those handbills hit the floor, Lyndon got mad, stalked out of the convention . . . and we pretty much controlled the convention."

Johnson, however, was not so quick to give up, according to other sources. Jubal R. Parten suggested to Johnson that he withdraw Bentsen's name and nominate another woman, one who had been loyal to the Democratic cause and had been active in party affairs. According to Voight, Johnson called her to meet with him about eleven or twelve o'clock in the evening. He told Voight that he didn't think he could win with Bentsen, but if she would consider running, he would back her.

Despite Johnson's persuasive techniques, Voight knew better than to challenge Randolph. The two women shared the same political base—the labor-loyalists. Voight declined, telling Johnson she had already pledged to Randolph and that if she challenged Randolph, she would be "run out of the state of Texas."

Realizing that even with Johnson's support and Connally working for her nomination that she could not muster the votes, Beryl Ann Bentsen withdrew from the race. Judge Jesse Andrews of Houston then placed Randolph's name in nomination, and it was seconded by Walter Hall. In his nominating speech, Judge Andrews cited Randolph's organizational techniques that had helped build the Harris County Democrats: "You ask anyone in Harris County—a banker, worker, Republican, or Democrat, who is the most successful. You get one answer, Frankie Randolph."

Randolph won—and the taste of victory was sweet, not only for her but for the Harris County Democrats. Randolph claimed victory for Texas Democrats in the upcoming elections and thanked her supporters: "I could never thank you enough, for this is the greatest honor a woman could have." Nevertheless, the attempt on the part of the Harris County Democrats to purge Shivers supporters from the SDEC failed, although J. Edwin Smith noted, "We won the battle considered by far the most important."

The fight between the liberals and Johnson had far-reaching effects and influenced Texas Democratic politics for years to come. Ball said that after Randolph had won as national committeewoman, he walked to the convention parking lot with John Connally. Connally said to him, " 'Well, Ed, you won this one. But you'll never win another one!' And he was pretty much right." Eventually, Johnson forgave Ball, but, as he revealed, "I had to go to Washington, get down on my knees, and ask for his forgiveness."

Bowing to Johnson and Rayburn's request, the liberals helped elect Connally chair of the delegation to the national convention. Johnson felt that if he was going to the convention as a "favorite-son delegate, he needed his own man as chairman of the delegation."

Voight remained skeptical of the SDEC's ability to remain loyal to Democratic candidates. As director of organization of the party's campaign committee, she put out a newsletter to county leaders, calling for "fair play and good faith" and warning them that "the SDEC is still in the hands of Republican-Shivercrats who are prepared to use the power and prestige of their office to lend support to the Republican party in November. . . . The Shivers dominated convention in the past has been unscrupulous in ignoring the selections of the Senatorial Districts and naming their own selections to perpetuate the machine of the governor."

Over the summer, other Democratic leaders tried to preserve and promote the victory they had won at the convention. The Harris County Democrats slated a dinner honoring the new committee members at the Rice Hotel, and Walter G. Hall was instrumental in setting up radio and television interviews for both Skelton and Randolph. He also was in the forefront of the reception planned by the Galveston Democracy Club, scheduled for July 18, 1956, at the Galvez Hotel, and attended by "all loyal Democrats in South East Texas."

Accepting the inevitable, Johnson did not attend, but sent "cordial greetings" and told Democrats he looked forward to "seeing you and working with many of you in Chicago." Ralph Yarborough was also not in attendance, but telegraphed his best wishes to Frankie Randolph and Byron Skelton, "This Democrat is with you tonight in spirit if not in flesh."

Despite his "cordial greetings," loyalists didn't have to wait until the national convention to feel Johnson's wrath. As Kathleen Voight recalled, "Lyndon gave and he took, but he was Texas." Although Johnson had won the right to lead the delegation to the Democratic National Convention, he was furious at attempts by the labor-loyalists. When loyalists arrived at the September convention, the so-called "governor's convention," it wasn't the governor's power they had to fight—it was Johnson's.

With John Connally working behind the scenes, Johnson had moved his allies onto the credentials committee, and Frankie Randolph and other delegates from Harris County were denied seats at the convention. Loyalists were outraged, not only over Randolph's ouster but also because conservatives had purged Kathleen Voight as director of party organization and membership. Writing in the *Texas Observer*, Franklin Jones noted that Randolph "had to sit outside in a cowbarn all day. This was a contemptible breach of personal courtesy and an unheard of affront to one of the state's two highest party officers. Mrs. Randolph chose to represent the wishes of the Houston Democrats instead of trading out those wishes to Johnson and Rayburn. They could not take this defeat in good grace. It was the kind of crude, small-time, and vindictive stroke for which Johnson is famous."

Billie Carr, with the HCD, recalled: "They threw us out, but they told Mrs. Randolph she could sit on the platform as she was the Democratic national committeewoman. She said, 'No, thank you. If my people are in the cowbarn, I go to the cowbarn, too.' She went to the cowbarn and a lot of us followed her. For many years, we judged people's loyalty as to whether they were in the convention hall or in the cowbarn."

Jubal R. Parten, Texas oil man who supported many liberal causes and was close to Rayburn, protested to the Speaker. Rayburn told him to take his feelings to Johnson, no doubt being certain of Johnson's reaction. Knowing that Randolph and the Harris County delegation had every legal right to be seated, Parten confronted Johnson, telling him in no uncertain terms: "Mister, you're making the biggest mistake of your life here . . . allowing Frankie Randolph to stand out there in the foyer and refusing to let her delegation be seated."

Johnson retorted that Connally was in charge and that Randolph and her "gang of 'red hots' should have stayed in line last May." Parten warned both Johnson and Rayburn that they were both "making wounds that will take many years to heal." And he was right.

In a letter in the *Observer*, addressed to the "Loyal Democrats of Texas," however, Randolph thanked them for their "firm stand on principle" and told them not to be discouraged by losses to the conservatives for they had gained "a great moral victory." She further assured them that she would stand at their side and encouraged them all to work to elect Stevenson and Kefauver at the national level.

As national committeewoman, Randolph went to the national convention. Creekmore Fath had a box seat as he had worked with the national committee in past elections, and he said that both of them "pretty much ignored Lyndon." He was certainly not their favorite-son candidate. For many labor-loyalists, Lyndon Johnson would not get their vote in 1956; nor would he in 1960.

Frankie Randolph never forgave Lyndon Johnson for opposing her, and, according to Ball, "carried a chip on her shoulder the rest of her life. I don't blame her. He really tried to do her in. He really tried to beat her."

Billie Carr also remembered Frankie's animosity toward Johnson. According to Carr, years later when Johnson was vice-president, he called Randolph on the telephone, greeting her by her first name. "Who gave you permission to call me Frankie?" she boomed. Then, without so much as a goodbye, she hung up the phone.

EIGHT

Organizing the Democrats of Texas

Frankie Randolph's election as national committeewoman gave her the position and clout to move to the forefront of Texas Democratic politics. Her work with the Harris County Democrats and her superior organizational skills had paid off. Eddie Ball felt that from the time of her election, she was "pretty much in charge of the loyal Democrats in Texas." She had contact with every county leader, and a new organization, the Democrats of Texas, developed a "good deal of political power in the state." Where their contacts paid off was in getting Ralph Yarborough elected to the United States Senate.

By 1956 the land and insurance scandals had taken their toll on Shivers's administrations, with Insurance Commissioner J. Byron Saunders resigning and Land Commissioner Bascomb Giles gaining a prison term. In the wake of the scandals, the loyalists knew their perennial candidate, Ralph Yarborough, had more than a fighting chance to win the governor's office. Yarborough had developed his name identification across the state and had gained strength as a campaigner, while Randolph and the Harris County Democrats, along with other loyalist groups across the state, stood firmly behind him.

His conservative challenger was U.S. Senator Price Daniel, who had been active in the fight over Texas's claims to its tidelands. Returning to Texas to hew steadfastly to the conservative line, Daniel proved a formidable opponent for Yarborough. Still more challenging were the reactionary candidacies of West Texan J. Evetts Haley and former governor W. Lee "Pappy" O'Daniel. Both O'Daniel and Haley spoke out against integration, while Daniel spoke out against both the CIO and the NAACP.

Yarborough took his fight to the people, stressing teacher pay raises, strengthening public-health programs, an anti-lobby law, and old-age pensions. Unfortunately, O'Daniel and his "Hillbilly Band" siphoned off many longtime Yarborough supporters, although Yarborough campaigned alongside an East Texas musical group, the Cass County Coon Hunters. Daniel played into the sideshow-style campaign tactics by having Fess Parker (television's Davy Crockett and a University of Texas graduate) campaign for him at the Alamo.

Randolph was in the forefront of those calling for Yarborough's election, telling loyal Democrats: "We must elect a Democrat governor, and I know but one in the race and that is our great friend, Ralph Yarborough. . . . The one we have to defeat is the bosom friend of Shivers and has always been—Price Daniel."

When the primary votes were tallied, Yarborough and Daniel were forced into a runoff, with conservative forces solidly aligned behind Daniel. Former governor Shivers endorsed Daniel, while "Pappy" O'Daniel threw his support to Yarborough. A serious blow to Yarborough's campaign in Houston occurred when a write-in vote for an African-American candidate siphoned off votes that Yarborough and the Harris County Democrats had counted on.

Despite ardent campaigning on the part of the loyalists across the state, and especially in Harris County, Daniel squeaked to victory with a margin of some 3,000 votes, many of which were contested. After the votes were counted, boxes of Yarborough votes were discovered in trash heaps.

Although he had suffered a heartbreaking loss, Yarborough had made significant gains statewide, carrying 146 of the state's

254 counties, and sending his progressive message across the state. To loyal Democrats, he still seemed the beacon of hope, the candidate most likely to reach back to the state's populist past and bring it into the progressive future.

If Yarborough's dreams of becoming governor of Texas died in 1956, a call for a special election to fill the U.S. Senate seat vacated by Daniel gave hope to the loyalist Democrats to build on Yarborough's strong showing in the governor's race. One of Governor Daniel's first acts in January 1957 was to appoint conservative businessman William A. Blakely to his seat in the Senate, until an election could be held.

To loyal Democrats, Blakely was anathema, a continuation of the Shivers-Daniel conservative politics which spelled no progressive reform for Texas. With the special election to be held in April, the labor-loyalists went to work. Precinct-by-precinct organization was called for, the very type of campaign organization that Randolph and the Harris County Democrats knew how to build.

Other contenders jumped into the race, including Republican Thad Hutcheson and Martin Dies, a U.S. congressman and chairman of the House Un-American Activities Committee. Dies was an ineffective campaigner and a man abhorrent to Speaker Sam Rayburn. Johnson, Rayburn, and Daniel tried to coax Dies to withdraw from the race to give way to the candidacy of Texas's lieutenant governor, Ben Ramsey. But Dies held firm.

The state legislature was in session, however, and conservative House members were out to "gut Yarborough" and to change the rules of the electoral process. Texas election law clearly stated that the victor in the special election had merely to gain the most votes, not necessarily a clear majority. According to Governor Daniel, however, this election was an "emergency," and House member Joe Pool introduced legislation mandating a runoff election if no one candidate received a majority.

Intense and acrimonious lobbying on the issue led to the House narrowly passing the measure, but it met opposition in the Senate, where many members eyed higher office and feared they might face a special election with changed rules. Some simply did not like the lobbying tactics being used, while others

were sensitive to charges of corruption in the Shivers administration and feared being tarred by the same brush.

Even conservative newspapers spoke out against the proposed changes in the election rules and the attempts to destroy
Yarborough's candidacy. The measure failed in the Senate, and
the two candidates began campaigning in earnest. In addition to
Randolph and the Harris County Democrats, Yarborough had
the support of the newly organized Democrats of Texas, Eddie
Ball's dream made reality and the organization that loyalists had
been calling for since 1952.

The Democrats of Texas were in the forefront of campaign
organization, planting stories in newspapers across the state,
while the *Texas Observer* ran feature stories, editorials, and news
stories about the candidate, the campaign, and its issues.
Numbers of the loyalist wealthy, including Randolph, Jubal R.
Parten, Walter Hall, and Fagan Dickson, gave generously to the
campaign.

In the April election, when Dies and Hutcheson split the
conservative vote and Yarborough won with 38 percent of the
vote, the new junior senator from Texas was generous in his
thanks. He wrote to Major Parten: "Through one hard campaign after another you threw your continuing support on the
side of good government in Texas and by your dedication you
have played a major role in the victory we have won." Of
Randolph, he later wrote: "Mrs. Randolph's support and en-
couragement more than that of any other one person was a
major factor in my going to the U.S. Senate."

Loyalists in Texas had won a major victory, and no group
celebrated more than the Democrats of Texas, with the group's
chairperson, Frankie Randolph, announcing that Yarborough's
win was "a great victory for the dedicated Democrats." Organized in response to the treatment that the loyalists had received
in Fort Worth, the Democrats of Texas had garnered criticism
early in their organizational stage, and no one came under more
criticism than Randolph.

As early as January 1957, the *Houston Post* had carried a
story that officials of the Democratic party would ask Randolph
to resign as national committeewoman over the issue of chairing

an organization formed outside party lines. Randolph announced that she had no intention of resigning from the national committee and told the *Post,* in no uncertain terms, that the charges were false and was an attempt to "try to intimidate me and other Democrats in Texas from participating in the organization we have formed."

The *Post* alleged that Speaker Rayburn was one of the officials who would call for Randolph's resignation, and the Speaker answered the charges in typical Rayburn manner: "It's a goddam lie!" When Lyndon Johnson was asked to make a statement, he merely noted, "I have no comment!"

Democratic National Committee Chairman Paul Butler called the *Post* story "totally untrue, unjust and embarrassing" and reiterated that "no one on the Democratic National Committee would try to unseat her." Randolph checked with lawyers regarding possible libel actions against the newspaper, and the issue—but not the controversy—blew over.

In February, Randolph and the Democrats of Texas planned their first convention to be held in Austin, with Randolph budgeting $10,000 for the meeting and appointing Creekmore Fath, Bob Eckhardt, and Kathleen Voight to a planning committee to make arrangements.

Fath had come up with the plan for the Democrats of Texas to be organized along the lines of the Democratic Clubs in California, and Randolph, attending a meeting of the national committee, told the press the group had the sanction of the national committee. The group's purpose was "to work for the platform and the candidates of the Democratic party."

The *Texas Observer* in its May 9 editorial commended the work of the organization: "If DOT is nothing else, its success in separating the Republican-leaning people from the Democrat-leaning people in the heretofore chaotic and divided 'Democratic Party of Texas' would justify its presence for it is the division of Texans now along perceptible lines of opinion about public policy that is enabling citizens to focus their judgment on public men and through party political action. "

At the convention held at Austin's Stephen F. Austin Hotel, with 1,000 Democrats from 106 counties in attendance, Randolph was elected the permanent chairperson. Ralph Yarborough introduced her as "the greatest Democratic national committeewoman in Texas history." Addressing the convention, Randolph told the group that the Democrats of Texas were "a new force to be reckoned on in Texas politics," and that the organization had "developed directly from the treatment we received at the September convention in Fort Worth."

With a verbal slap in the face to the Shivercrats who had voted Republican, she stated the group's goals: "We're going forward until we, the Democrats, will control the 1958 convention." She lambasted the members of the State Democratic Executive Committee, who, she claimed, "have by deliberate inaction abjectly betrayed the best interests of Texas," and called on the delegates, working through their precinct organizations, to control the group.

The DOT began its work with a newly adopted insignia, a star with a large "DOT" in its center, and with a newsletter, the *Democratic Reporter,* linking its members to the steering committee. The first issue of the *Reporter* carried a cartoon by member Bob Eckhardt, showing two professional politicians, with one saying, "Don't look now, but I think the people are trying to steal the party again."

The DOT began its organizational and fundraising work for the national Democratic party out of Fath's office in Austin's Littlefield Building, with Randolph calling for volunteers to go into the various counties to conduct organizing workshops.

The State Democratic Executive Committee struck back at the organizational impetus of the DOT by hiring J. J. "Jake" Pickle as its statewide director of organization. Pickle was anathema to backers of Yarborough, for his Austin public relations firm, Syers, Pickle & Winn, had produced "The Port Arthur Story" for Shivers's campaign against Yarborough.

The DOT sounded its war cry, "No Nickles for Pickle," and resolved that no funds collected by their group should go to the SDEC. In September the steering committee, responding to a resolution by its vice-chairman, Alex Dickie, voted to send all funds to the national committee and that "no funds would be retained by any faction in the state." The committee also adopted a party code, a restatement of the loyalty oath, and Randolph was designated to present the proposal to the SDEC at its next meeting.

September also found Randolph and SDEC Chairman Jim Lindsay crossing swords on the party code in a closed-door session at the regional conference of Democrats meeting in Oklahoma City. The Texas group earned the ire of National Democratic Chairman Paul Butler, who cited Texas as the only state in the nation with such a "serious intraparty rift." Randolph spoke out in defense of the Democrats of Texas, stating that the group "was fighting for three rights, the right to vote, the right to have our votes counted, and the right to have our votes counted right."

Randolph restated her claims at a meeting of the DOT in El Paso, to which the *El Paso Times* editorialized: "If that group (DOT) should gain control of the Democratic Party in Texas and read out of the party all those Texans who call themselves Democrats but who voted for Dwight D. Eisenhower in 1952 and again in 1956, it will be the swan song for the Democratic Party in Texas."

Randolph then waged war on Pickle, who charged that "extremists" were behind the organization of the DOT. Touring the state, Randolph charged that Pickle's claims were false and that members of the DOT steering committee were chosen by caucus of its members. Further, Randolph claimed that Pickle and Governor Daniel were carrying on "the same old Dixiecrat machine built by Shivers" and charged that Pickle "has always been a henchman for Allan Shivers." She added that "The state . . . committee has hired Jake Pickle to the tune of $15,000 a year to organize the state for the Dixiecrats. He is a very smart propagandist—Allan Shivers trained him, so you know he knows all the tricks."

Calling on Democrats to "sponsor a party registration bill— if they are Democrats," Randolph noted the election of Yarborough to the U.S. Senate as a symbol of the growing strength of Democrats loyal to the party. "They fear us—we have grown stronger each year."

The DOT launched an aggressive campaign against the payment of a poll tax as a requirement for voting in Texas, an issue that Fath had long favored. On November 19 the *Dallas Morning News* carried a story in which the SDEC claimed erroneously that members of the armed services could not vote and the disabled did not have to pay poll taxes. DOT member Jean Lee charged in the *Observer* that someone on the SDEC had "goofed" or had "published erroneous information" on the poll tax situation.

Randolph went even further, claiming in the DOT newsletter that the SDEC statement to the press was a deliberate "subversion of democracy," and that it "betrays either gross stupidity or an intentional scheme to hold down poll tax payments by misleading, misinforming, and confusing Democrats." Frankie Randolph was inclined to believe it was the latter.

By the end of 1957, the Democrats of Texas, under Frankie Randolph's leadership, had made significant organizational strides, presenting a strong challenge to the State Democratic Executive Committee. They had made their point on the issue of a party code, and Randolph was poised, ready to throw down the gauntlet in the wake of her nemesis Lyndon Johnson's bid for another run for the presidency as Texas's favorite son.

In December, at a Farmers Union convention in Abilene, Randolph reacted to calls for "harmony" by the SDEC, telling the farm group: "I'm going to fight for you. I'm not going to be intimidated. I'm going on trying to organize the loyal Democrats. They tell us to harmonize with the Dixiecrats. Now what have they ever done for us? They pretend to be Democrats and haven't supported the Democratic nominee for president since [Wendell] Wilkie. Those are the people who will tell you we do not need DOT."

When a reporter for the *Abilene Reporter-News* asked Randolph her opinion of Johnson's proposed candidacy in 1960, she "uncorked an unequivocal disapproval," going on to chastise Eisenhower for having run for reelection after his heart attack. With Johnson recovering from his own heart attack, her challenge to him was clear: "It is criminal of any person to run for office after having a major heart attack. . . . I am not pro-Lyndon . . . I am not a Lyndon Johnson person. I am not interested in electing another heart case president. . . . We elected a man who had a heart condition—should we go out and elect another one? I'm against it."

Johnson was furious and retaliated in print, noting his grueling record of speeches and meetings while in West Texas and thanking his friends "for prayers that sustained me in the dark hours when death clouds were hovering around."

The second act of the Frankie Randolph–Lyndon Johnson battle was on.

NINE

"Tugboat Annie"
of Texas Politics

*F*rankie Randolph took seriously her role as national committeewoman and the party fundraising that was an inherent part of the job. Democrats such as Walter Hall moved to see that she got full credit for her fundraising efforts.

Hall pledged a sustaining membership of $400 to the party, sending a check for $200 to National Chairman Paul Butler by way of Randolph. In a letter to Butler, he noted that "Frankie Randolph is keenly interested in the support of our National Party, and when she called me about helping the Party, I could no longer delay it. I am sure you understand the pride we take in the leadership we are getting from Frankie Randolph, and we are confident that from your Committee she will receive support in the difficult problems she is trying to handle." When Hall gave his check to Randolph, he told her to be sure that his letter accompanied it. "I want him [Butler] to know full well that you are providing the leadership for the real Democrats in this state," he told her.

Randolph was indeed besieged with "difficult problems," many of them concerning the DOT's continued call for a "Code of Ethics" within the party and her ongoing feud with Lyndon

Johnson. The verbal blows with Johnson at the Farm Bureau meeting were not the only ones that she and the Senate majority leader exchanged. The *Houston Post* carried a story in which Johnson deplored the failure of the United States Vanguard missile and the success of the Russians' *Sputnik*. The *Post* reported that Johnson advised "junking the forty-hour work week" in order to challenge the Soviet Union in a space race.

Randolph fired off a letter to Johnson on December 13, 1957, criticizing him for seeming to blame the nation's "fine working force" for the failure of the United States to launch a successful missile before the Russians did so. Johnson replied that he had not advocated doing away with the entire forty-hour week, but only that relative to the production schedule of ICBMs.

In a reference to Adlai Stevenson's defeat in his latest presidential bid, Randolph castigated Johnson even further: "Our relative recent disdain for what some politicians have called 'eggheads' seems surely to have contributed more to our lag in scientific development than has the 40-hour week. . . . Your junk the 40-hour week plan . . . sounds like the using of a grave issue to achieve political acclaim as a latter-day prophet."

Randolph's defense of the labor force was well timed for the AFL and CIO had recently combined, and the Texas labor organization was giving support and financial backing to the DOT. Labor's Council on Political Education supported the DOT's call for a "Code of Ethics" that would bind party members to votes for Democratic candidates and provide a strong party registration law. In addition, Jerry Holleman and Fred Schmidt, top-ranking officers in the Texas AFL-CIO, and Robert Bryant, president of the railroad brotherhoods, began serving as members-at-large on the DOT's executive board.

Labor's active participation in the DOT gave the group increased political clout, but also increased the animosity toward the group among Texas conservatives. With conservatives in the majority on the State Democratic Executive Committee and with the group strongly in the Rayburn-Johnson-Daniel camp, opposition focused on the DOT's call for a "Code of Ethics."

A series of letters distributed among lobbyists and special interest groups by conservative attorney Preston A. Weatherred, a former general in the Texas State Guard, challenged the state's conservatives to "close ranks" against the DOT. According to Weatherred, if the DOT were to gain its aims, it would "wipe from the Texas statute books most labor laws." Weatherred went on to warn: "Then would come repeal of the Texas right-to-work law. . . . Texas will cease to be a haven of individual enterprise and individual liberty."

The DOT stood by its call for a "Code of Ethics" within the state Democratic party, with Governor Price Daniel calling on the group to disband, labeling it an illegal extraparty group, and demanding that it cease using the word "Democrat" in its title. No doubt the organization was often confused with the State Democratic Executive Committee, and the "Code of Ethics" was anathema both to the governor and the SDEC.

Intraparty squabbling over the issue resulted in a wrangle between Randolph and SDEC Committeewoman Marietta Brooks. Sam Wood, political editor for the *Austin American-Statesman*, labeled the skirmish a contest between "Tugboat Annie" (Randolph) and the "Dimpled Darling" (Brooks) of Texas politics.

The first round of the Brooks-Randolph bout took place when Brooks, the vice-chair of the SDEC, close friend and strong supporter of Lyndon Johnson's, and ardent worker in Johnson's campaigns who often accompanied Lady Bird Johnson on speaking tours, called on Randolph to apologize to the SDEC for having on two occasions said that some of its members were disloyal to the Democratic party. Randolph replied in writing, but her answer failed to receive wide distribution by the media.

In a letter to Creekmore Fath, dated January 23, 1958, Walter Hall related that "Frankie's letter to Mrs. Brooks and her later press release have been terrific. However, the newspapers in this area have not given good coverage. . . . I am wondering if, for publicity purposes, it might be wise to challenge Price or Jake to have a joint statewide TV debate on the merits of a Code of Ethics. . . . If they would be crazy enough to agree to it, I will contribute $100 to the cost of the broadcast."

Although a television debate never materialized, the fracas between Brooks and Randolph played to gleeful reporters prior

*The Carter children: Aubrey,
Frankie, W. T. Jr., and Agnese.*
—Molly Luhrs Collection

Frankie and Aubrey Carter.
—Molly Luhrs Collection

Maude Holley Carter and W. T. Carter.
—Molly Luhrs Collection

Number 14 Courtlandt Place—the W. T. Carter residence.
—Molly Luhrs Collection

W. T. Carter—East Texas timber baron.
—Molly Luhrs Collection

W. T. and Maude Holley Carter superimposed before Niagara Falls.
—Molly Luhrs Collection

Frankie Carter, on "Black Bess," rides with a friend.
—Molly Luhrs Collection

Frankie Carter as a young woman.
—Molly Luhrs Collection

Agnese Carter as a young woman.
—Molly Luhrs Collection

A pensive Frankie Carter.
—Molly Luhrs Collection

Frankie Carter in bonnet with maids at the No-Tsu-Oh Carnival the year
Agnese Carter reigned as queen.
—Molly Luhrs Collection

Deke Randolph, his brother, and his mother Jane with their English cousins,
including Marguerite Radclyffe Hall.
—Molly Luhrs Collection

Deke Randolph in the Naval Air Corps,
World War I.
—Molly Luhrs Collection

The Randolph family crest.
—Molly Luhrs Collection

Frankie Carter and Deke Randolph's wedding party—June 14, 1918.
—Molly Luhrs Collection

Frankie Randolph in her younger years.
—Molly Luhrs Collection

Young equestrians Aubrey and
Jean Randolph.
—Molly Luhrs Collection

Aubrey Carter
Randolph.
—Molly Luhrs Collection

Jean Randolph at a Houston horse show.
—Molly Luhrs Collection

Wedding party of Jean Randolph and David Longmaid.
—Molly Luhrs Collection

Frankie Randolph's sisters, Jessie Carter Taylor and Lena Carter Carroll.
—Molly Luhrs Collection

Agnese Carter Nelms and Lena Carter Carroll at Camden.
—Molly Luhrs Collection

*Deke Randolph (right) and James A. Baker with portrait of
Houston financier Jesse Jones.*
—Molly Luhrs Collection

Deke and Frankie Randolph.
—Molly Luhrs Collection

*Billie Carr—Frankie Randolph's
political protegé.*
—Molly Luhrs Collection

Frankie Randolph in her rose garden.
—*Houston Post*

A smiling Frankie Randolph relaxes at the beach.
—Molly Luhrs Collection

Frankie Randolph and Creekmore Fath lead the loyalists in a bolt to Austin's Barton Springs.
—Molly Luhrs Collection

Frankie Randolph and Ralph Yarborough congratu-
late each other on winning an election.
— Photo by Richard Pervin

Ralph Yarborough greets Adlai Stevenson on a campaign tour through Texas.
—Molly Luhrs Collection

Cartoon of Frankie Randolph taking the liberal axe to the members of the Conservative Democratic Club.

— Texas magazine/Houston Chronicle

The Harris County delegation to the Texas House of Representatives, 1959. Among the group are Criss Cole, Roger Dailey, Bob Eckhardt, Dean Johnston, Bill Kilgarlin, Clyde Miller, J. Charles Whitfield, and J. Ed. Winfree.

—Molly Luhrs Collection

Frankie and Deke Randolph with their daughters,
sons-in-law, and grandchildren.

—Houston Post

Above: *Randolph holds great-grandson James*
Randolph Armstrong with daughter Aubrey and
granddaughter Molly Armstrong.

—Molly Luhrs Collection

Left: *Frankie Randolph with granddaughters*
Molly and Frances.

—Molly Luhrs Collection

Frankie Randolph—
the political years.
—Molly Luhrs Collection

Molly Luhrs at Camden.
—Molly Luhrs Collection

Frankie and her daughter Jean.
— Houston Press Archives, Houston
Metropolitan Research Center

to the opening of the SDEC meeting on February 1, 1958. Brooks took up the governor's call for the group to disband, charging that the DOT was in violation of the Texas election code, as its name was similar to that of the regular party organization. Randolph was quick to respond, countering with a slap at Brooks's support of Republicans in past elections: "I don't believe good Democrats need to sit still for being lectured on Democratic Party support by people who went charging off on 'Womanpower for Eisenhower.'"

In his column "Ladies Night," Wood described Marietta Brooks as a "conservative . . . a striking brunette . . . more at home in the social tea parlor than the free-swinging political circus." Of Randolph he wrote: "In the woman's world of democracy on wheels she is rough, tough and two-fisted. She asks no quarter and gives none. She's not afraid of Elephants. In fact she is a real Elephant tail-twister when you apply the word Elephant to its place in politics . . . she has taken on just about every lion in Texas politics. . . . Her pet hate is Allan Shivers."

By the time the SDEC meeting opened at Austin's Driskill Hotel, nineteen reporters hovered around Randolph and Brooks, and cameras clicked every time the two women came in close proximity to each other. Brooks issued a call for all Democratic women to sit down with her over a cup of coffee and "let's be ladies." Randolph ignored the invitation.

In addition to the Brooks-Randolph brouhaha, controversy continued to swirl around the DOT's call for a "Code of Ethics," which Randolph presented to the SDEC. She received an ovation from the group and answered Governor Daniel's charges that the DOT was a splinter group and that the name caused confusion and was misleading. In her statement, Randolph maintained: "I am a Democrat and I'm a Texan, and the members of DOT are Democrats and they are Texans. So why should they not call themselves DOTs. . . . The DOT will be the majority group in Texas when we have a [party] registration bill and remove the Republicans from our primaries."

Mrs. E. T. Robbins of Orange called for the code to be considered. John Peace of San Antonio proposed it be sent to the resolutions committee, and Fagan Dickson offered a substitute plan allowing the code to be sent to the committee, but requiring that a report be returned in writing within thirty days. Dickson's motion was adopted unanimously.

In a luncheon address, National Committeeman Byron Skelton added to the acrimony, castigating the loyalist organization: "DOT . . . is not authorized by law, it's not approved by the national committee, it has no place in our set up, we do not need it. The DOT is causing confusion, disunity, duplicity, controversy, animosity, among Democrats." He echoed the call for the DOT to disband so that the Democrats could unite behind Sam Rayburn and Johnson and go to the 1960 convention "as one man."

Concerning the legality of the group, Fagan Dickson retorted: "If they're not illegal, they're entitled to do what they want as Democrats." Randolph went even further. When asked if she would disband the group, she replied: "Indeed not. For one I couldn't if I tried. For another, why should I, when we have 'em on the run?"

It was obvious that the DOT's call for a "Code of Ethics" was dead, so far as acceptance by the State Democratic Executive Committee. The group did agree to study Governor Daniel's plan to abolish precinct conventions in favor of directly elected precinct delegates. The DOT made some headway when the SDEC voted to study the advisability of a party registration bill; however, in a direct challenge to the DOT, the SDEC voted to look for ways to prevent "usurption *[sic]* of the party name."

If Randolph thought her confrontation with Brooks was a challenge, she met still another one in March. She was in Washington on national committee business when she received an invitation from Senate Majority Leader Lyndon Johnson to drop by for a chat. Johnson had never ceased running for president, and, as 1960 was the year he felt he would win the nomination of his party, it was important to him to touch base with all factions of the Democratic party in Texas.

Jim Mathis of the *Houston Post* reported that the two long-time enemies conversed for an hour, primarily discussing the *Observer,* which, according to Mathis, "has plagued the senator." The *Observer* commented that "Johnson quite likely got over his position that with his past record of liberal accomplishments, he'll bow to no extremists." Randolph didn't comment on the meeting, but her animosity toward Johnson continued and would be manifested at the 1960 Democratic convention.

Back in Texas, Randolph continued her speaking on behalf of the DOT, often defending the group against charges of domination by its labor membership. Speaking to the Travis County Democrats in Austin in April, she declared that the group "truly represented the people of the state" and repeated her accusation that members of the State Democratic Executive Committee were "Republicans and Dixiecrats." She referred to the governor as "Republican Price Daniel."

Randolph backed up her defense of the DOT by listing its accomplishments and telling the Travis County organization that there were similar groups in twenty-two states and that the national committee did not oppose any of these. She called on the SDEC to support the party registration bill, stating, "I do not believe that Republicans should continue to pose as Democrats."

Randolph's use of her position as national committeewoman to promote and defend the Democrats of Texas won her a legion of enemies among conservatives in the Democratic party—a legion who began calling for her removal from the national post. However, others applauded her efforts, and her name became synonymous with loyalty to the Democratic party. One mark of her growing celebrity within party affairs came in April 1958, when the Wharton County Young Democrats passed a resolution urging her to throw her hat into the turbulent Texas political ring—and to run for governor of the Lone Star State.

TEN

Victory at
the Precincts

If Lyndon Johnson was gearing up for a presidential race, Texans were getting ready for an equally important governor's race that pitted Governor Price Daniel, running for a second term, against Texas's first Hispanic gubernatorial challenger. Henry B. Gonzalez, the state senator from Bexar County, posed a liberal challenge to the conservative governor, while U.S. Senator Ralph Yarborough was running for a full term in his own right.

With two candidates at the top of the ballot that seemed ideally suited to loyalist forces around the state, Frankie Randolph called the annual meeting of the Democrats of Texas for May 31, 1958, in Austin. Not only was the group primed for the state-wide elections, the Harris County Democrats, the strongest arm of the organization, was "flexing its muscle," having replaced many of the conservative members on the county executive committee with members loyal to the party and sympathetic to the goals of the HCD and the DOT.

The situation in Harris County was an ideal one for the HCD to make its move. Harris County had one senatorial seat and eight legislative seats, with the senatorial seat open and six of the eight legislative seats open, just waiting for loyalists to file.

And, with Randolph and the HCD's support, file they did. Never had Harris County seen so many loyalist names on the ballot for the Texas legislature.

Robert W. Barker filed for state senator with the support of the HCD, and two incumbents, Criss Cole (running for the Texas House of Representatives in Position 7) and J. Ed Winfree (running for Position 5), had the group's endorsement. Also filing with HCD support were Dean Johnston, former instructor at the University of Houston and the *Texas Observer's* advertising and circulation manager, for Position 1; Bob Eckhardt, a labor attorney and the chairman of the Harris County Democrats, filing for Position 2; Clyde Miller, active in the railway brotherhoods, for Position 3; Bill Kilgarlin, a law student at the University of Texas and president of the Young Democrats of Harris County, for Position 4; Roger Daily, former assistant attorney general and active in Ralph Yarborough's campaigns, for Position 7; and attorney J. Charles Whitfield for Position 8.

The Harris County Democrats were determined to move their loyalist candidates to the statehouse, and Randolph's work in precinct organization over the years paid off during this campaign. Bill Kilgarlin recalled that "her work in organizing precincts certainly played an important role in getting us elected. By motivating workers and supporters' activity in an effort to gain control of the [Democratic] party (and we did, electing Woodrow Seals as county chairman of the party, and electing a substantial number of members to the county executive committee and winning control of the county convention), she indirectly aided the election of each of us."

While the Harris County Democrats were gearing up for legislative races, Randolph announced that the guest speakers for the DOT convention would be U.S. Senator Ralph Yarborough and District Judge James Sewell, a survivor of many of the loyal Democrats' battles. In mid-May local DOT groups met countywide to choose delegates to the statewide meeting. Dean Johnston presented a resolution calling for party registration, and the group endorsed Yarborough for reelection to the Senate. They also endorsed former state senator George Nokes for lieutenant governor and HCD member J. Edwin Smith and Sarah Hughes of Dallas for the Texas Supreme Court.

Significantly missing from the endorsement list was the name of Henry B. Gonzalez for governor, although his name was mentioned several times throughout the meeting. The matter of whether to endorse would occupy the DOT county meetings prior to the statewide meeting. The matter would be in the hands of the steering committee, scheduled to meet on May 30, as the DOT constitution specified that only the steering committee could make the determination to endorse.

The *Texas Observer* reported that a movement to forego endorsements had been developing among executive board members, with some members feeling that Gonzalez "should not be linked with Yarborough through DOT." With delegates siding both ways, hot arguments ensued. The *Observer* speculated that the Bexar County delegation, led by County Commissioner Albert Pena, would endorse Gonzalez, but Creekmore Fath, the DOT's secretary-treasurer, told the *Observer* he felt that it would be best to leave endorsements to the county groups, noting that, "Once we win one state convention, then DOT will be able to step out on candidates."

Gonzalez himself commented in the *Observer* that he didn't believe in "putting his friends on the spot," and noted: "All I want is their vote. I would not initiate or request endorsement; it would have to come from within. . . . I realize some think a Mexican-American might hurt a ticket. . . . And nobody wants to bet on what they think is a loser. Organizations naturally want a winner."

Further, the candidate wrote a letter to Randolph offering to forego an endorsement, if it would create dissension within the group. He told the *Observer* that Randolph and Bob Eckhardt "were concerned that if DOT does not endorse him 25 percent will be angry, and if it does, another 25 percent will be angry."

Governor Daniel also challenged the DOT, charging the group with "political manipulation" and "sowing the seeds of disunity." He threatened to lead the fight to regain precinct convention control for the conservatives. Then, on the eve of the group's convention, Sam Wood, political editor of the *Austin American-Statesman*, ran an article on the DOT, which appeared

not only in the *Statesman* but in all the newspapers of the
Fentress chain. Charging that Randolph was the "front for the
DOT" and Yarborough the "Kingpin of the DOT," Wood
claimed that the group was an alliance of four minorities: the
AFL-CIO, NAACP, the Texas Farmers Union, and "ultra-liberal
Latin voters."

The story had an even wider distribution when Johnny
Jones of the Whitley Company printed 20,000 copies of the article and offered it for sale at three dollars per hundred or twenty
dollars per thousand. Governor Daniel accepted the offer, buy-
ing copies of the article and giving them to the lobby for wide
distribution. The Texas Manufacturers Association also bought
copies and mailed them to its entire membership. By July, the
article had been so widely circulated around the state that Randolph felt compelled to write to Texas religious leaders warning
them about the article and of "racist propaganda and pamphle-
teering" on the part of the governor.

True to predictions, when the DOT members met in Austin
on May 31, they voted not to endorse candidates, with the steering committee feeling that the organization's central purpose
was party reform and victory at the state conventions. The *Observer* reported that the DOT did not turn away from Gonzalez
but invited him to speak "with electrifyingly successful results."
Nevertheless, the fact that some DOT members were not ready
to accept a Hispanic candidate, nor willing to endorse him as a
gubernatorial candidate, may well have weakened the organization. The *Observer* sagely counseled the group, "DOT would have
been bold and wise to endorse candidates, including Gonzalez."

After the DOT convention, the battle continued to discredit
the group, with National Committeeman Byron Skelton sending
a letter to former members of the Democratic Advisory Council,
claiming that some members of the DOT were "trying to create
the impression that the DOT is a successor to the old Democratic Advisory Committee. . . . Of course, all of you know that is
not true." Frankie Randolph knew that Skelton's remarks were
aimed at her and fired off a rebuttal letter to the former DAC
members, outlining the goals of the organization as dedicated
to seeing that only Democrats participate in "the affairs of the

Democratic Party," and that the rights of "locally, lawfully selected delegates to Democratic conventions shall not be violated."

Randolph continued to maintain that the DOT was not a splinter group: "Let this much be understood clearly. It is not for Price Daniel to say if we are a minority or a majority. It is not for Byron Skelton to say. Democrats will determine that issue face to face, in convention assembled. "

In July, speaking in San Antonio to a bar convention, Governor Daniel struck back, condemning the DOT as "an outlaw minority group," and beginning a concerted effort among political leaders to have Randolph removed as national committeewoman. The governor claimed that she "could not get along with any of the duly elected state officials."

Randolph and the Harris County Democrats tasted a sweet victory in August, when their candidates landed in runoffs, and Kilgarlin won his two-man race outright. They were assured of a liberal voice in the Texas House of Representatives, and began gearing up to win other seats in the runoffs. Randolph was quick to praise the workers who had campaigned fervently for the liberal candidates: "This is the victory of the precinct workers—the voluntary precinct workers . . . it is almost unbelievable that you could do what you did with all the money poured out and all the propaganda against you."

Randolph was right; the victory was impressive. The Texas Manufacturers Association had backed the Harris County Taxpayers Committee in mounting conservative candidates and had poured money into the campaign, running their general counsel and lobbyist, Charles Murphy, for the Texas Senate against the HCD's candidate, Robert W. Barker. In the runoffs in late August, all the HCD-backed legislative candidates won. The only defeat was that of J. Edwin Smith for the Texas Supreme Court by a narrow margin.

Smith, one of the original founders of the Harris County Democrats, felt that Randolph and her close associates within the group were the cause of his defeat and that Randolph opposed him as the two had differed over the election of District Judge Ben Wilson. Smith said that "the Harris County Democrats, except Frankie's close faction, supported me. Even though

I had stood with her to be Committeewoman in opposition to Lyndon Johnson, she would not then help me out of spite for my blocking her desire to defeat Judge Ben Wilson. . . . [I] have always felt that had Frankie supported me as I did her for Committeewoman, I would have won."

Despite the wins in Harris County and the reelection of Ralph Yarborough to the United States Senate, the loyalist forces within the Democrats of Texas had failed to gain control of the party machinery at the state Democratic convention, held in San Antonio on September 9, 1958. Their candidate for chairman of the convention, Judge Jim Sewell, lost to the Johnson-Rayburn-Daniel candidate, Frank Ikard.

In his keynote speech, Governor Daniel reiterated his demand that the DOT remove the word "Democrat" from its name. Daniel also declared war on the DOT by orchestrating the refusal of allowing two duly elected nominees to be seated on the State Democratic Executive Committee, because they were members of the DOT. The two nominees had been chosen in senatorial district caucuses in Waco and San Antonio.

So blatant was Daniel's move that both Rayburn and Johnson sent telegrams protesting the move, seeing it as a challenge flung in the face of the DOT, whose members Johnson would need in his pursuit of the presidency in 1960.

Before a vote could be taken, Daniel adjourned the convention and ordered the lights and air conditioning turned off. Undaunted, Frankie Randolph led a group of a thousand disgruntled delegates to the Gunter Hotel, hoping to find Senator Yarborough to hear their protests. The governor's actions led Randolph to castigate the "ruthless, cynical, selfish political machine that has dominated Texas politics for a generation," and to rally the DOT to promote its precinct work. With the governor continuing to hammer away at the group's use of the "Democrats of Texas," however, in October 1958 the DOT bowed to the inevitable and changed its name to the Democrats of Texas Clubs.

ELEVEN

"The Hardest Working Democrat"

*F*rom the moment that Frankie Randolph was elected national committeewoman, conservative forces had been trying to get her removed. As early as January 1957, stories circulated that a "hush-hush" effort was being made to replace her. Conservative Democrats in Texas complained to the national committee that she was using her efforts only to support the Democrats of Texas and not the party as a whole.

Charges were brought that Randolph had not turned over funds from a Harris County Democratic campaign dinner to the national committee. However, this issue was resolved when Chairman Paul Butler explained that all funds from the dinner were safely in the hands of the national committee. However, during 1958 and 1959, conservatives continued their move to have Randolph removed as committeewoman in favor of someone more in tune with their political views.

In addition, Randolph had garnered controversy by supporting the candidacy of Hattie Mae White, the first African American since Reconstruction to be elected to the board of trustees of the Houston Independent School District. According to Chris Dixie, Randolph supported White "under the table" for

74

in 1958, many of the members of the American Federation of Labor refused to support African Americans for political office.

Campaigning as an African-American woman for a seat on the board was difficult. White remembered it as the "first time blacks and whites had ever worked together on an organized campaign." When she won, a cross was set afire on her lawn and air-rifle pellets shattered the windshield of her car.

Dixie believed that Randolph gave White financial funding for the campaign, but the Harris County Democrats did not endorse her. However, many of the members supported her, and when she won, White made a point on election night of coming by to thank Randolph for her support.

During the summer of 1958, rumors of an intense effort to remove Randolph grew to such a point that Creekmore Fath sent a report to the DOTC steering committee on August 22: "Mrs. Randolph has done a magnificent job for the Democrats in this state. We cannot let her down. In order to see to it that she is reelected National Committeewoman, and that Democrats are on the delegation to the National Convention in 1960, we have to intensify our efforts now."

As the time for the September state convention approached, newspapers were reporting the move to oust the committeewoman, with Allen Duckworth of the *Dallas Morning News* noting that confidential sources had revealed that a resolution demanding her removal was being "drawn" and would be presented at the convention.

National committee members, however, were only nominated by state committees and were elected by the national committee. Nevertheless, conservative forces continued to charge that she could not get along with members of the State Democratic Executive Committee, and Texas conservative politicians explored legal means of removing her.

As national committeewoman, Randolph had a podium for her agenda, and in December 1958 she warned Texas Democrats about inroads made into conventions by the Freedom in Action Committee, an offshoot of the John Birch Society. She explained that "very few people are aware of the danger of that group," and noted that the FIA was importing both organizers and workers into Houston and that Harris County was one of their principal targets.

Randolph also continued to speak out on national issues, and in December 1958 expressed her support for Illinois Senator Paul Douglas for the Democratic nomination for president in 1960. When asked how she felt about the potential candidacy of Lyndon Johnson, she stated: "Lyndon has said he's not a candidate. Let's leave it at that."

In February Johnson had, indeed, announced that he would not run, and many of his supporters felt he should not give up his post as majority leader for a shot at the presidency. After months of hedging, however, in April Johnson became a candidate, and his candidacy proved to be an issue that threatened to split liberals and labor.

In an extraordinary move, the 1959 session of the Texas legislature voted changes in the Texas election law favorable to Johnson's candidacy. Bills were introduced that moved the primaries from July to May, allowing for only one set of precinct and county conventions. Moving the primaries to May allowed Johnson to be nominated for reelection to the U.S. Senate and also allowed him to be a presidential candidate.

Another change in the election laws was music to liberal ears. After years of pushing for a party pledge, liberals applauded when the legislature decreed that when a voter cast a vote in a primary or attended a primary convention, his or her poll tax receipt or exemption certificate would be stamped with the name of the party each had voted with. This law effectively prevented voters from later participating in the affairs of another political party.

Some liberals saw the handwriting on the wall and began making deals with Johnson; others, who held firm, would feel the long arm of Johnson. He was well known for putting his grudges into action. Bill Kilgarlin, then a member of the Texas House of Representatives, said that liberal members of the House were presented with a dilemma. "Because of Mrs. Randolph's violent opposition to Johnson, many of us did the politically unwise thing" and voted against the legislation. The bills passed overwhelmingly, and Johnson declared war on liberal House members.

Johnson, however, knew he would need the support of liberals during his campaign, and named Woodrow Seals as co-chairman of the Kennedy-Johnson campaign. When Johnson took office, he saw that Kennedy appointed Seals as United States attorney for the Southern District of Texas. However, John H. Crooker, Jr., his co-chair for the campaign, extracted a pledge from Seals that he would not appoint either Kilgarlin or Dean Johnston, another House member and strong supporter of Mrs. Randolph's, to positions in his office. According to Kilgarlin, Seals told Crooker that it was easy to take that pledge, for Johnston was not an attorney and Kilgarlin was still in law school.

For determined liberals who had done battle with Lyndon Johnson for years, however, there was no compromise. Two of these were Frankie Randolph and Creekmore Fath. Fath stated simply: "There was no way I could have made peace with Lyndon. This went back a long way, back to the 1940s. I thought Lyndon was a scoundrel." Randolph also cut no slack with the majority leader. At one point, Johnson asked her, "What can I do for you, Mrs. Randolph?" Looking him straight in the eye, she replied, "Nothing."

By fall 1959, party politics in Texas was at a fever pitch. Randolph attended the western caucus of the national committee in Washington and reported to the Harris County Democrats that the committee members "except for the Dixiecrats" want a "liberal nominee [for president] and want Congress to pass liberal legislation." She further warned: "The nominee must not be a middle-of-the-roader."

With Adlai Stevenson still the first choice for liberals across the nation, Lyndon Johnson expressed doubt that Stevenson, a "two-time" loser, could carry the Democrats to victory, and Walter Hall doubted that he would get the nomination. By this time, Randolph had reverted to the Stevenson camp. She told the *Texas Observer*, "I'm a Stevenson woman. . . . I think he's the greatest statesman that we've ever had," but declined to endorse anyone, keeping her options open.

In July a group of non-labor Texas liberals had met in Abilene, and the "Stevenson for President" movement was launched in Texas, with Stevenson's campaign manager listing Randolph as one of his "Texas Democrats for Stevenson." As the time of the 1960 convention approached, however, she began to think that Stevenson could not win, and switched her allegiance to John F. Kennedy, no doubt seeing him, as many liberals did, as a viable alternative to Johnson.

Creekmore Fath recalled that Eleanor Roosevelt and Agnes Meyer, journalist and wife of the publisher of the *Washington Post,* continued to support Stevenson. Roosevelt called him to encourage him to stand by Stevenson, and Fath came to Houston to talk to Randolph about the campaign. Randolph told him: "Creek, this is nonsense. We love Adlai, but Jack Kennedy is going to get the nomination. I'm going to be for Jack Kennedy."

As the campaign intensified, rumors continued to circulate that Randolph would be replaced as committeewoman at the national convention in 1960. In September 1959 the *Houston Post* reported that there was a move to oust Randolph and that she faced a "battle for survival." The newspaper story cited the fact that "Conservatives have vowed to replace her. The scrap may break into the open as early as the May 7 precinct conventions." The article also cited the fact that Randolph was "out of step" with conservative leadership and failed to get along with National Committeeman Skelton.

In October former president Harry Truman visited Texas to rally the Democratic party to regain the White House in 1960. When Truman spoke in Dallas, Randolph appeared on the platform with the former president, Speaker Sam Rayburn, Johnson, and Ralph Yarborough. Truman also spoke to the executive committee of the DOTC, with Randolph introducing him as the "greatest living Democrat." Randolph also announced to the group that their meeting would be a working meeting, adding, "You know what they say about me in Harris [County]: the only word I know is 'work.' "

Later in the month, Michigan governor G. Mennen Williams, considered both a presidential and vice-presidential candidate in 1960, visited Houston and was honored at a reception hosted by liberal Democrats, with Randolph in the group. Williams told liberals that he was dedicated to seeing that the Democratic candidates for national office were both "liberal and dynamic," and said of Lyndon Johnson: "He is a super legislative technician. . . . But he is not liberal enough."

In November 1959, Loretta Craft of the Women's Auxiliary of the International Association of Machinists presented Randolph with its Good Citizenship Citation for 1959, noting that she had "performed great public service" and had "maintained wonderful dignity and calm" in the face of unfair and dishonest attacks against her.

Speaking at the dinner, hosted by the Harris County Democrats, at Houston's Rice Hotel, Senator Ralph Yarborough lauded her as the person who had held Democrats "feet to the fire," and was "by far the hardest working Democrat in the state of Texas." Yarborough used the occasion to warn the audience against the FIA and all reactionary factions and called for Texas Democrats to work together at the national convention, noting the fact that 1960 would be "one of the tough years for the liberal Democrats."

In his speech, Yarborough noted the moves to oust Randolph as national committeewoman and lauded her as "the greatest Democratic national committeewoman in the history of Texas." He went on to point out: "Not only has she invariably held the Democratic position when it was in the public interest, but she has forced a number of other so-called Democrats to keep faith with our party of the people." Yarborough encouraged all Harris County Democrats to "join Frankie Randolph and go to work in the precincts."

When the Democrats of Texas met in convention in Harris County on February 19, 1960, the battle lines were drawn for the national convention. Randolph opened the session, calling on all Democrats to participate in precinct conventions, and stated that with their help, "This year can be, must be and shall be the year of Democratic victory." Although he was not at the convention, Senator Yarborough sent a letter noting that if Texas was to be in the Democratic column, it would be because of "you loyal DOT Democrats."

Yarborough's letter pulled no punches, warning the organization against "June Democrats becoming October Republicans. . . . Beware those Judas goats who led us to slaughter in

1952 and 1956 who now tell you they are good, loyal Democrats and your sole organizers for the 1960 national convention. "

Also missing from the convention were numbers of the faithful that the DOTC had recruited over the years. Only five hundred members showed up, one-half of the number that had appeared at the 1958 and 1959 conventions. It was apparent that Johnson's candidacy or the increasing strength of labor within DOTC had made significant inroads into the group's membership.

Labor leader Otto Mullinax of Dallas proposed a resolution in opposition to Johnson's candidacy; however, he withdrew the resolution after the labor delegates banded together to prevent any official criticism of Johnson. Jerry Holleman, head of the Texas AFL-CIO, stated that if a formal resolution criticizing Johnson were passed, labor would split from the group. Both Randolph and Fath agreed not to impose any official criticism of Johnson; Randolph told the group that the best strategy was "not to mention Johnson at all," pointing out that Johnson was vain and would be "most annoyed by not being mentioned."

While the organization pledged to support Randolph for reelection as committeewoman, Johnson stated that he could work with Randolph if she wanted him to. Randolph rallied members with words aimed at conservative efforts to disband the group: "You will go on fighting after betrayals and more betrayals by our so-called Democratic leaders. You never lose heart. . . ."

The *Texas Observer* took labor to task over its threat to split from the Democrats of Texas Clubs, noting that "Texas labor's leadership is first dedicated to labor, second to DOT. A division is developing. It may be arrested; it may not. . . ." The *Observer* went on to state that "Texas liberals mistrust him [Johnson]" and warned that "either the Texas liberals oppose Johnson in his home state . . . or make a deal with him."

Johnson continued to draw support not only throughout the state of Texas, but from a number of Southern governors. Many of the liberal faithful joined with Woodrow Seals in supporting Johnson, including Dickinson banker Walter Hall. In explaining his support of Johnson, Hall told the DOTC members: "Johnson has a good voting record in the Senate. We might feel, some of us at least, that he votes right for the wrong reasons, but he's got a good voting record."

Senator Yarborough stated that he would support Johnson if the Texas delegation was instructed to vote for the majority leader, and Senator John F. Kennedy said that he considered Johnson to be his most formidable rival.

Conservatives, meanwhile, were determined to win control of the party apparatus through winning precinct and county conventions in order to control delegates to the state convention. Writing in the *Houston Chronicle*, political reporter Walter Mansell noted: "A lot of conservatives do not like Johnson any more than do a lot of liberals. But they probably would not buck Johnson too strongly because they would have little place to go."

The conservative effort focused on precinct organization, the exact strategy that had built both the Harris County Democrats and the Democrats of Texas Clubs. The strategy, put into effect across the state, worked equally well for conservatives and had dire consequences for both the DOTC and Frankie Randolph.

TWELVE

Defeat

While Lyndon Johnson's presidential race gained increasing national media attention, Texans geared up for a gubernatorial election. With Governor Price Daniel a strong favorite to win, the DOTC mounted no liberal candidate, but strongly supported liberal Don Yarborough for lieutenant governor against conservative Ben Ramsey. Although Ramsey won, Yarborough made an impressive showing, gaining 631,689 votes to Ramsey's 834,516. Yarborough proved a very viable candidate that the liberals could look to in the future.

With Daniel in the Governor's Mansion and closely aligned with the Johnson campaign, Frankie Randolph could expect no letup in the attempt to remove her as national committeewoman. In addition, by March 1960, she was again at loggerheads with the State Democratic Executive Committee, calling on National Committeeman Byron Skelton and SDEC chairman J. Ed Connally to plan a fundraising dinner to pay off the Democratic party debts. She also served notice on the SDEC that she, as national committeewoman, had not been informed of an SDEC meeting held on March 14.

On March 15, Billy Goldberg, state Democratic committeeman from Harris County, presented the issue of the loyalty oath before the SDEC, and his motion was rejected. In addition, Walter Hall presented a petition signed by 50,000 Texans to submit a referendum in May to the voters on abolishing the poll tax. The committee also refused his request.

Randolph fired off a letter to J. Ed Connally criticizing the committee for failing to act on the resolutions, and the SDEC chairman told the press: "Frankie Randolph's latest political outburst is merely another attempt by the DOT splinter group to divide our party."

In May, as precinct and county conventions were held across the state, Texas liberals and conservatives went to war. The issues were the loyalty oath, Johnson's presidential candidacy, and nomination of Randolph for a second term as national committeewoman. On each of these issues, the liberals would experience significant losses.

In Travis County, Johnson's home district, the majority leader was the overwhelming choice in the precincts, but liberals rallied to gain support for the loyalty oath at the county convention. Capitol newsman Stuart Long led the liberal forces against Johnson, and conservatives opposed Long for county chairman, as his loyalist caucus had endorsed Randolph.

In Bexar County, Randolph received support as national committeewoman in only thirteen precincts, but liberals held firm at the county convention and elected liberal Albert Pena, Jr., as chairman. The group would go to the state convention under instructions to vote for Johnson, but also would vote to support the loyalty oath and Randolph.

It was in Harris County, however, that liberal-conservative battles were most prominent. Although conservatives voted not to support any presidential candidate, the Harris County Democrats voted to reject any resolution on the part of Johnson for president, but to support the candidate of the party.

In the midst of both conservative and liberal bolts at the precinct levels, Randolph experienced a significant defeat that would presage others to come. In her precinct, she failed to win election to the county convention and was thus not a delegate to the state convention. However, as national committeewoman, she held one-half vote at the national convention and was very much a presence at both conventions.

At the county convention, on May 20, loyal Harris County Democrats bolted, demanding that Randolph be reelected national committeewoman and that Creekmore Fath be chosen as national committeeman to replace Byron Skelton. The group also voted to support the presidential nominee of the Democratic party.

Randolph vowed "On to L.A." and predicted "a good rumping group of loyalists from Texas" would be at the national convention. Judge Jesse Andrews, a longtime supporter of Randolph's, but by 1960 solidly in the Johnson camp, asked Randolph if she would forego a bolt if the county delegates designated her as their choice for national committeewoman again. Randolph refused, insisting that at the national convention Texas delegates be released from supporting Johnson after the first ballot and calling on the group to make Ralph Yarborough head of the Texas delegation. When the convention delegates refused to back the loyalty oath, the bolt was on.

As the state convention approached, Governor Price Daniel, noting the advances made by moderates and conservatives, told the media that he "wouldn't think" that Randolph would be reelected as national committeewoman, commenting that the post would go either to Hilda Weinert (whom Randolph had replaced) or to Marietta Brooks.

In the meantime, the Democratic National Committee called on their state conventions to pass general loyalty resolutions, and prior to the state convention held in Austin in June, the SDEC prepared a resolution stating, in part: "It is understood that the Delegates to the Democratic National Convention, when certified by the State Democratic Party, are bona fide Democrats who have the interests, welfare and success of the Democratic Party at heart, and will participate in the Convention in good faith, and therefore no additional assurances shall be required of the Delegates to the Democratic National Convention in the absence of credentials contest or challenge."

For many liberals, including labor leaders, this served as a viable alternative to the personal loyalty pledge that the DOTC called for; however, Randolph, Fath, and others stood firmly for the loyalty pledge and refused to compromise.

When the state convention opened in Austin in June, the Johnson bandwagon was on a roll. Labor leaders swelled the ranks, having accepted the SDEC pledge as sufficient. As labor leaders Jerry Holleman and Fred Schmidt of the Texas AFL-CIO stated, they felt that party loyalty had been their goal, and that "goal we feel was largely accomplished." The DOTC call for a loyalty oath was defeated by a vote of 2,252 to 40.

Liberal defeats at the precinct and county level led to the defeat of the loyalty oath and to the vote to replace Randolph as national committeewoman. As she was not a delegate, she, along with many of the DOTC members, were meeting at Austin's Barton Springs when the nomination of Weinert was approved, replacing her as national committeewoman.

A number of delegates refused to bolt the convention, with Maury Maverick, Jr., pleading earnestly with the Bexar County delegation to bolt. However, Albert Pena and G. J. Sutton sided with the moderates on the issue of the loyalty pledge, voting against a bolt in exchange for a pledge from Johnson and Daniel to help elect liberal legislative candidates from San Antonio over Republican opponents.

Randolph expressed the frustration and disappointment of the Barton Springs liberals, telling the press: "As you know, not a county rumped. . . . There were, I think, ten counties that voted with us on the resolution [the loyalty oath]. But they did not rump. You can't be a rump delegation if you haven't been joined by anybody inside who has rumped." Randolph led her "depleted and defeated" DOTC members home, but vowed to continue to work for party loyalty.

Many liberals blamed their defeat on Fath and Randolph's refusal to compromise on the loyalty issue. One reporter summed it up as her "stubbornness . . . her unswerving, uncompromising, unrelenting insistence on purity in the Democratic Party in Texas. . . . No Eisenhower Democrats, no Dewey Democrats, no Willkie Democrats—and no Johnson Democrats."

Others felt it was labor's defection that had caused them to lose so badly. Still others would trace the downfall of the liberal group to a split in its membership when members failed to endorse Henry B. Gonzalez for governor. Nevertheless, they had waged a battle against seemingly impossible odds, and the loss was a significant one. The DOTC went down in defeat, and the state had lost its most outspoken national committeewoman.

But the Democrats of Texas had fulfilled a useful purpose in the state, keeping alive the liberal agenda, backing liberal candidates, and consistently calling for party loyalty. Ronnie Dugger would later recall, in a fitting epitaph to the group, that "in Houston Mrs. Randolph led what may have been historically the most powerful progressive movement in Texas since the farmers' Populism of the preceding century."

When the Democratic National Convention opened in Los Angeles on July 10, 1960, Paul Butler, the national chairman, gave Randolph and Creekmore Fath a box next to Eleanor Roosevelt and Agnes Meyer. Johnson was furious with Butler, a strong supporter of Kennedy's, when he gave Randolph sixty tickets and distributed tickets liberally among Texans known to support Kennedy. "I know one thing," Johnson told the press, "that gallery is not going to be stacked in favor of me."

Fath remembered that Randolph distanced herself from the Texas delegation with its hoopla, its "Ladies for Lyndon," and its determined support for Texas's favorite-son candidate. She took no part in its caucuses or deliberations, going to the floor only to cast her vote. Chris Dixie recalled, however, that Randolph was very prevalent, "spreading the poison against Lyndon." Working the floor against Johnson, she was joined by other members of the DOTC, including Fath, Kilgarlin, and Dean Johnston.

From her box on July 13, Randolph witnessed Sam Rayburn placing Johnson's name in nomination for the presidency and the balloting in which Kennedy won the nomination handily on the first ballot. Texans had come together to support Johnson's candidacy, but with Kennedy's strong call for civil rights heading the ticket, Texans soon split into factions once again. Governor Price Daniel stated that the Republicans might well carry Texas in the upcoming election. Daniel also announced that he would support the ticket, but would not work for it.

Not so for Frankie Randolph. She was a Democrat, and even

with Lyndon Johnson on the ticket, she would work for a Democrat in the White House. After all, Kennedy was a liberal, the Democratic party had adopted a civil rights plank, and the thought of Republican Richard Nixon in the White House posed a larger problem for her than Lyndon Johnson as vice-president.

Billie Carr, who worked side-by-side with Randolph in many of the fights against Johnson, remembered that she "really knew how to roll with the punches. Defeat made her stronger. She was always ready for the next fight. She just believed so strongly in what she was doing." And what she was doing at that time was working with the Harris County Democrats to see that John F. Kennedy was elected president of the United States.

Bob Eckhardt, chairman of the HCD, called a meeting of the executive committee of the group that voted unanimously to send a telegram to the Kennedy-Johnson campaign offering their service "in carrying Harris County for you." The Harris County Democrats threw their support solidly behind the ticket, and on a rainy August 29, 1960, the group sponsored a Kennedy Ladies Tea, with Lady Bird Johnson, Eunice Shriver, and Ethel Kennedy attending. Prominent among the Texas Democratic women attending were Jean Daniel, wife of Governor Price Daniel, and Frankie Randolph.

In September, Kennedy campaigned in Texas, with Governor Daniel introducing him from the steps of the Texas State Capitol. When Kennedy's plane touched down in Houston on September 12, a unified group of conservatives and liberals greeted the candidate. Among them were Randolph, Chris Dixie, Bob Eckhardt, Senator Robert Barker, Jesse Andrews, and Jim Yancy, general counsel for the Texas Manufacturers Association.

The group moved on to the Houston City Coliseum to be joined by Mayor Lewis Cutrer and Democratic Congressmen Jack Brooks, Bob Casey, and Albert Thomas. From there, Kennedy would move on to address the Greater Houston Ministerial Alliance on the subject of separation of church and state and to defend his stance as a Catholic running for the office of president of the United States.

The Democratic faithful crowded the coliseum to get a glimpse of the man who was destined to carry a liberal agenda to the White House, and when the candidate was introduced, they rose to their feet to salute Kennedy. The second largest round of applause, however, was for the woman who had been soundly defeated as national committeewoman from Texas— Frankie Randolph.

THIRTEEN

The Conscience
of the Party

$\mathcal{D}$espite Democratic efforts, the Republican party had been building in Texas, and Lyndon Johnson's vacated seat in the United States Senate proved the battleground for Democrats to present a strong challenge to the growing strength of Texas Republicans. When Governor Price Daniel appointed conservative William Blakely to Johnson's seat, the challenge to liberals was clear. Blakely, who had challenged Ralph Yarborough for his U.S. Senate seat, was an enemy to liberals.

Rumors circulated in political circles that former governor Allan Shivers might run for the seat; Shivers was yet another conservative whom liberals abhorred. And then the floodgates opened. State Senator Henry B. Gonzalez announced, pledging his wholehearted support for Kennedy's New Frontier, and hoping to garner all of Texas's liberal votes. When Texas Attorney General Will Wilson and "progressive-moderate" U.S. Congressman Jim Wright of Fort Worth threw their hats into the ring, a flood of other Democrats announced, with Blakely stating his intention to campaign for the seat he held.

When former state legislator Maury Maverick announced, the liberal vote was split. There was no question in the minds of

Randolph and other members of the Harris County Democrats as to which candidate they would support. Maverick had been with them throughout the Texas liberal-conservative battles and had backed the liberal agenda as a state legislator. In addition, his father, former Congressman Maury Maverick, Sr., had been one of the leaders of the Texas loyalists throughout the battles of the 1940s.

Then Republican John G. Tower announced his candidacy. Tower, a professor of government at Midwestern University in Wichita Falls, had been chosen by the Republican State Convention to challenge Johnson for his Senate seat in the November election and had pulled a substantial forty percent of the vote against Johnson—not enough for a win, but enough to make him a viable candidate for the contested Senate seat.

Wilson and Wright could be counted on to pull conservative votes from Blakely, but Republicans had been steadily eroding conservative Democratic strength, particularly in the Dallas and Houston metropolitan areas. In addition, with both Gonzalez and Maverick in the race, the liberal vote was up for grabs.

Randolph called former members of the DOTC to a meeting to garner support for Maverick, and Harris County Democrats worked to bring out the vote. Liberals knew they had to muster their support behind one candidate, but the choice was a difficult one. Writing in the *Observer* of February 23, 1961, Ronnie Dugger bemoaned the choice and its results: "For friends and associates in what is loosely called the liberal movement in Texas to start now also choosing between each other because of the choice each must make between Maverick and Gonzalez ought not to be necessary, but it is happening, and it is becoming the basis for a general calamity for liberalism."

Like many liberals, including labor leaders and Randolph, Dugger concluded that "Maverick could beat Tower, and Gonzalez might not." He went on to explain the *Observer's* endorsement: "Maverick has firmer control of his emotions, makes better speeches, is better organized, has a better chance to win, and would make a greater senator."

Randolph added her own endorsement, writing in the *Texas AFL-CIO News*: "Maverick is the best man to help our Senator

Ralph Yarborough achieve his legislative goals for Texas. Maverick is the best man to implement reasonable and prudent ideas of his own in the world's greatest legislative body. . . . Texas will be proud to send another Maverick to Washington."

With both the conservatives and the liberals split, however, when the vote was counted on April 4, 1961, Republican Tower led the field with a commanding 31.5 percent of the vote, followed by Blakely's 18.3 percent. Trailing Wright and Wilson were the liberal candidates, Maverick with 10.2 percent and Gonzalez with 9.3 percent of the vote.

As the figures show, had the liberals solidified their strength around one candidate, a liberal candidate might well have made the runoff and presented a formidable challenge to Tower. As it stood, liberals were faced with a dilemma—vote for a conservative Democrat who had opposed them at every turn or vote for a Republican. A third option also presented itself—not to vote at all.

Since the 1940s Texas liberals had been striving to wrest the Democratic party machinery from conservatives. Their defeat at the statewide convention proved to them that if they were to control the party the only way was for conservative Democrats, who had consistently voted Republican over the years, to switch to the Republican party.

That was the reasoning worked out in the news stories and editorials of the *Texas Observer,* with its publisher Ronnie Dugger and editor Willie Morris urging liberals to vote for Tower in hopes of establishing a true two-party system in Texas. Nevertheless, the decision was a difficult one for many liberals to make. Unused to sitting out elections, faced with the dilemma of having no candidate to carry their agenda, and unable to support a Republican, many were torn in their loyalties. One was Frankie Randolph.

Pondering the choices, she sent out a letter under her personal signature that was widely distributed among former DOTC members, Harris County Democrats, and loyalists around the state. In her letter, she said: "Blakely cannot be considered the Democratic nominee. . . . Blakely was decisively rejected the only time he sought the nomination . . . against Ralph

Yarborough in 1958." Determining that she could not vote for a Republican, she stated, "I will do one of two things on May 27: either write in the name of a good Democrat or go fishing."

Many liberals followed her advice and some did indeed "go fishing," including former candidate Maury Maverick. Gonzalez threw his support to Blakely, but other liberals, including Chris Dixie, voted for Tower, supporting the two-party system and reasoning that in later elections they could muster the strength to defeat Tower. They figured wrong. Tower would hold his Senate seat until 1984, when he stepped down, having overseen the building of a strong two-party system in Texas and the sweep of the South by Presidents Nixon and Reagan that would carry Texas by the 1990s into the Republican column.

While liberals were celebrating Kennedy's slim margin over Nixon in the state and his victory in the presidential campaign, they were also rallying support to send liberals to the Texas legislature and to the governor's office. When Lyndon Johnson's Senate seat had been vacated, a number of moderate and conservative Democrats had urged Johnson's campaign manager and longtime political cohort John Connally to run. Connally, however, chose not to run, and accepted a post as Kennedy's secretary of the navy.

Now, Connally felt, was the time to enter elective politics in Texas. In December 1961 he announced that he would run for governor. To many Texans, Connally was an unknown, though liberals knew him well from the battles at various conventions and as a key figure in the Rayburn-Johnson-Daniel clique that had done battle with them for years. In June 1961, a poll showed Connally with only one percent of the vote, largely due to lack of name identification throughout the state.

A flock of conservatives jumped into the gubernatorial race, including Governor Daniel, who belatedly decided to seek a fourth term; Attorney General Will Wilson; Marshall Formby, former chairman of the Texas Highway Commission; and right-wing Gen. Edwin Walker, an avowed fighter against communism. The liberals found their candidate when Don Yarborough, supported solidly by the Harris County Democrats, entered the race.

In the *Observer* of December 15, 1961, editor Willie Morris commented on the former Johnson campaign manager as governor of the state: "Connally's candidacy gives us only a sense of monumental boredom. He offers the same mild remedies and pale nostrums undergirded by the same apathetic popular front, the same lackadaisical stance against a two-party system. "

In January, Ronnie Dugger also denounced the conservative candidates, bringing up the issue of party loyalty and castigating Connally for refusing to endorse Stevenson in 1952 and Daniel for backing Eisenhower. Dugger went on to point out that Don Yarborough was far and away the best candidate, having "surrounded himself with advisors who are known and trusted liberals." Dugger also noted Yarborough's support by labor in his race for lieutenant governor against Ben Ramsey. But for Dugger, the best reason to vote for Don Yarborough was the fact that the liberal candidate had "a vote getting name and a vote getting style."

Although the DOTC was inactive, in March 1962 Randolph called a meeting of the executive committee of the former group to solidify liberal support behind Yarborough. "I'm going all out for Don Yarborough," she told the press, and noted that liberals were inspired and more active since Kennedy's election. She also energized the Wednesday Club, a group of forty to eighty liberals who gathered at the Houston *Observer* office under Randolph's supervision, aided by Kitty Peacock and Mary Beech.

The Harris County Democrats were also inspired to work for a liberal candidate for the Texas House of Representatives. Randolph was prominent on the campaign committee, helping to organize African-American voters, when a fledgling politician, Barbara Jordan, ran for Place 10 on the ballot. Since 1959, when students at Texas Southern University staged sit-ins at lunch counters in Houston's downtown stores, the African-American community in the city had been actively involved in politics. Jordan seemed the most likely candidate to win a House seat.

Randolph had long been pushing for civil rights for African Americans. As Billie Carr recalled: "She was very strong on civil rights, and she had a way of working with minorities. We used to go out to meetings in black neighborhoods, and she had a real interest in seeing that integration became a reality. She knew that civil rights and civil liberties would make a difference in people's lives. . . . She became the conscience of the party."

Labor also had a vested interest in seeing that African Americans voted, and the Harris County Democrats had since the 1960 campaign been active in empowering African Americans. Chris Dixie described the initial efforts to meld African Americans into a voting bloc: "I went to the black YMCA and rented chairs to fill the basketball court. Only five or six blacks showed up. . . . We had cards for them reading BLOCK CAPTAIN— DEMOCRATIC PARTY in red, white, and blue. They agreed to go into the plants. Workers stopped them and wanted cards just like theirs. In three days time, we were mobbed with applicants for block captains. . . . We had the first block worker program and gave prizes for the best performing precinct judges."

Barbara Jordan had been one of those who had worked hard for the Democratic ticket during the Kennedy-Johnson campaign, and although the Democrats failed to carry Harris County, Houston's African-American community turned out the largest number of votes of any metropolitan area in the South, helping the Democrats carry Texas by a 50.5 percent majority.

Although neither the Harris County Democrats nor labor had ever supported an African-American candidate for the legislature, Chris Dixie thought the time was right and encouraged Jordan to run, telling her that the Harris County Democrats would support her financially. Although other liberal House candidates would win in 1962, Jordan suffered a heartbreaking defeat to Willis Whatley, drawing only 23 percent of the white vote countywide.

The gubernatorial race also proved disappointing; Don Yarborough lost a hard-fought runoff to John Connally by 26,250 votes. Connally outspent Yarborough by some $200,000 and made the race a classic conservative-liberal one, going on to beat Republican Jack Cox and winning the Texas governor's office. In 1964 Yarborough, once again solidly backed by the Harris County Democrats, challenged Connally, but the governor swept to victory, carrying all but two of Texas's 254 counties. To liberals, their best hope of winning a statewide gubernatorial race disappeared with Yarborough's 1964 defeat.

Political defeats were balanced by victories, however, and Randolph was energized, along with other liberals, by working to see that the Harris County Democrats sent one of their own, Bob Eckhardt, to Congress in 1967. After distinguished service in the Texas House, where he carried the liberal agenda, Eckhardt won a U.S. congressional seat and served until the 1980s, when he was defeated by Republican Jack Fields.

Billie Carr said that Eckhardt might well not have made it to Congress had it not been for the Harris County Democrats and the strong precinct organization that Randolph put into motion. According to Carr, "You couldn't even get Eckhardt to campaign. He was off in the woods one time, two weeks before election time. When he rode up in his jeep, [Randolph] asked, 'Where have you been? This is a campaign.' He didn't like to campaign, so the Harris County Democrats had to do all the work. However, he was a great Congressman. There was nobody better in Congress than Bob Eckhardt."

Randolph even had difficulty with her longtime admirer, Ralph Yarborough, on the campaign trail. Carr remembered that the Harris County Democrats had set a headquarters opening for Yarborough at four o'clock one afternoon. The candidate called and said he had a chance to speak to a club at four and wanted to come at two instead. When Carr told Randolph of the senator's change of plans, she said, "Oh, my God. Give me the phone." According to Carr, she called him up and said, "Senator, this is Mrs. Randolph. The headquarters opening has been set for some time. We've sent all the announcements. We've sent all the publicity. You need to be there at four o'clock, if you want to be there when the people are there. If you want to come at two, I'll just leave the key under the door, and you can let yourself in."

She hung up the telephone, but in a few minutes, it rang again and Carr answered. It was Senator Yarborough, who said, "Billie, tell Mrs. Randolph, I'll be there at four o'clock." According to Carr, Randolph was the one whom Yarborough listened to, and liberals thought the world of him: "Nobody had a better voting record in the U.S. Senate than Ralph Yarborough."

FOURTEEN

"Such an Inspiration"

John F. Kennedy's death in 1963 presented liberals across the state and the Harris County Democrats in particular with a dilemma. Their longtime foe, Lyndon Johnson, the man they had done battle with in convention after convention for control of the Democratic party machinery, was now president.

Chris Dixie, chairman of the Harris County Democrats, called a meeting of the executive board at Randolph's home. He felt that the group must decide whether to issue a statement of support for the president, and that they needed to present their resolution—if passed—to the entire membership.

"I went around the table asking each person what to do," he said. "Everyone agreed that we had no choice but to announce that we were going to support Lyndon as president of the United States. When I got to Frankie, she said, without blinking an eye, 'You've got no other choice.' "

Dixie sent out a letter to the membership, and the group met in the Grand Ballroom of the Rice Hotel. "We passed the resolution," he said, "and for the first time in the history of the Harris County Democrats, a resolution calling for the passage of the Civil Rights Act."

Since 1959, Houston's African-American community had been actively working for civil rights and for desegregation of city establishments and neighborhoods. Now the focus changed to electing African Americans to office, and Barbara Jordan's defeat for a seat in the Texas House of Representatives only increased their determination.

One Houston group had as its goal recruiting qualified candidates and supporting their candidacies. The Committee for Better Local Government, with Jordan serving on the steering committee and Randolph heading the candidate committee, went to work. One of the documents that the committee put out for community leaders and candidates was *How to Organize Your Precinct,* putting into writing the strategies that Randolph had championed since the 1950s.

Liberals still had difficulty in getting members elected to the State Democratic Executive Committee. Billie Carr remembered that in 1964 there was a push to get a liberal elected, and the first person nominated was Barbara Jordan. Governor Connally vetoed Jordan, as there had never been an African American on the committee; then Katie Dixie was nominated, but Chris Dixie vetoed her serving. Then Carr was nominated and vetoed. When Lyndon Johnson got the word, he called Connally and told him to put Carr on, because she was Mrs. Randolph's choice, and they needed the Harris County Democrats for their next campaign.

Despite the loss of two races for the Texas House of Representatives in 1962 and 1964, Jordan remained a highly qualified candidate. African-American and female, a practicing attorney with a superb voice, she had the backing of labor, the Harris County Democrats, and the African-American community. When, on June 15, 1964, the Supreme Court ordered that all state legislatures apportion both their houses on the sole basis of population, the Texas legislature reapportioned its legislative districts. The newly created Eleventh Senatorial District in Harris County encompassed Jordan's Fifth Ward and its boxes included those that Jordan had carried handily in both her races.

Jordan had been working as executive assistant to Harris County Judge Bill Elliot, but resigned the position to challenge J. Charles Whitfield, the dean of the Harris County delegation, for the Senate seat. Her first test was winning the endorsement of the Harris County Democrats, who had helped Whitfield in his races for the Texas House. Randolph backed her solidly, as did Chris Dixie, Bob Eckhardt, and Eddie Ball, and Dixie carried her endorsement by the HCD executive committee to the full membership.

Whitfield was enraged. He turned his wrath on Jordan during the race, antagonizing many of his supporters. The *Texas Observer* carried a ringing endorsement: "Even if Whitfield and Miss Jordan were equally qualified, the *Observer* would be for Miss Jordan for the larger reason, the need to break the race barrier in the still all-white legislature; but they are not equally qualified: Miss Jordan is better qualified. . . . She has better political judgment than Whitfield . . . and she's more liberal. The coalition of labor, the minorities, and the unattached liberals in Houston is backing her all-out. . . . Let us hope that Miss Jordan is elected."

And elected she was, winning over Whitfield by 64 percent of the vote, and with no Republican challenger. She had become the first African-American to serve in the Texas Senate since Reconstruction and the first African-American woman ever to serve in the statehouse.

Jordan's victory was cause for Frankie Randolph to celebrate, for she had backed Jordan since her first race. In addition, Randolph had worked assiduously for civil rights and to see that African Americans gained their rightful place in society. She, along with many other liberals, were determined to break the color barrier in elective politics and to end segregation.

Billie Carr, who inherited Randolph's mantle of leadership with the Harris County Democrats, worked closely with her and helped to instill the idea of civil rights and civil liberties throughout the group and the community. Carr remembered, "We would say, 'Don't do that that way because it's not right. It isn't right that people have to sit in the back of the bus. It isn't right that people can't drink out of a water fountain. It isn't right that kids go downtown with their mothers and can't use the restrooms.' There was something inherently wrong about that, and you could talk to people about that kind of injustice."

Randolph worked in a highly personal way to break down barriers, from the time she demanded that Houston's Shamrock Hotel admit African Americans. Throughout the 1950s and 1960s, politicians knew that Randolph could be found at her special table in the back corner of Rudi's, one of Houston's private clubs. Randolph decided to have lunch at the club when she was in the company of Cora Guerin, wife of Texas Southern University professor Nick Guerin.

When the two women, one Anglo, one African American, appeared in the doorway, the maitre d' came rushing over and announced, "I'm sorry, Mrs. Randolph. We don't serve blacks." Unperturbed, she shot back, "Well, you do now." The two women entered, ate lunch, and no one in the club made a comment.

Rudi's was also the scene of a contretemps that added to Randolph's legendary status in Houston society. Her granddaughter Molly Luhrs said that they were sitting at Randolph's table one afternoon, while two men, the only other customers, sat at a nearby table. Overhearing a remark that she found offensive, Randolph rose from the table, indignant in the extreme, and assaulted the man with her overstuffed purse. The long-suffering maitre d' came running, and calmed Randolph, but the victim was furious, vowing to sue his tormentor for assault. Letters and recriminations flew back and forth, but nothing ever came of the case.

Because of her stately presence and commanding voice, people were drawn to Randolph. Her presence made her seem tall, but actually she was a very short person. Carr remembered that, "When she came into a room, everyone noticed her. People were drawn to her; it was amazing to see the kind of attention she received." One of the reasons she was so memorable to many people was her eyes. "She had wonderful eyes, very penetrating," Carr described. "She also had an absolute way of reading people. She could see a person one time and tell whether that person was someone we could trust or a fly-by-night. She could evaluate people in a minute."

No one was ever in doubt as to how he or she stood with Randolph, and she never hesitated to speak her mind. When Dean Johnston was serving in the Texas legislature, having made it to the House with HCD backing, he received a telegram from Randolph, which must have astounded him: "Don't Do Anything Until Tomorrow: You Have Made Enough Mistakes Today." She served as mentor to Billie Carr, bringing her along in the political world, teaching her the ways of organizing precincts and garnering votes. Yet when Carr was elected chair of her precinct and the county convention, and came into the HCD office, shouting gleefully, "I won! I won!," Randolph looked at her and said, "Well, I never thought you would."

"She was one of a kind, there's no doubt about that," Carr said. Randolph always told Carr that people would accept her (Carr) as a liberal, because Carr had come from a union background and was married to a union man. She remembered Randolph reflecting on the difference in their backgrounds and their involvement with liberal causes: " 'It's okay for you to be a liberal Democrat, but people consider me to be a traitor. They say it's not in my personal best interest.' Mrs. Randolph would laugh and say, 'They hate me more than they do you.' "

By 1965, poor health was taking its toll on Randolph. She suffered from angina, with years of cigarette smoking and whiskey drinking compounding the problem. She gave up cigarettes, but to her friends' amazement, took up smoking cigars. Carr said that the two of them would go to Rudi's or other restaurants, and when Randolph had finished her meal, she would take out a long cigar. "The waiters would rush to light that cigar, struggling to keep straight faces. I know when they went back to the kitchen, they laughed their heads off."

Randolph was forced to give up many of her political activities, including her active participation in the Texas Organization of Liberal Democrats, a group founded by Dixie and others to focus on liberal issues and candidates during the 1960s. She wrote to Latane Lambert, the secretary of the organization, that she was retiring from all active political work and declined an invitation to attend a coffee for U.S. Congressman Jim Wright, telling Warner L. Brock that she was giving up meetings under doctor's orders. She added that she was not sure she would support Wright but was "looking at his record."

Undoubtedly, Randolph had been contemplating her retirement from the active political scene for some time. She wrote a letter to Eckhardt telling him that she planned to "go to the Piney Woods and rock in a chair and read . . . it is time for new blood to take over." Despite her retirement, she kept abreast of all political events and issues, bombarding Senator Yarborough with requests for material on bills pending before the Senate and writing letters advocating Texas liberals for appointments to government positions. Yarborough often asked for her help on Texas issues, sending her copies of his speeches, Kennedy's civil rights address to Congress, and articles from the *Congressional Record*.

On August 17, 1965, she wrote to him recommending Bill Ballew for a federal judgeship, and in the same month, the senator wrote to her asking for help in funding radio spots to fight against four-year terms for Texas governors. When the proposition was defeated, postponed for consideration until 1967, he wrote this thanks: "Again your early leadership inspired many others to lift up their hands and work. God bless you."

On August 15, 1966, she wrote to Senator Yarborough advocating Ed Cogburn for a position as federal district attorney, and Yarborough responded by saying that he felt the position should be filled from either Galveston or Nueces County, but if it were filled from Houston, he would add Cogburn's name to the list. He added a personal note: "We loyal Democrats never told you how concerned we were when you went to the hospital this year. It is a great relief to see that you're out in the pine trees and feeling so much better. . . . You have been such an inspiration to those of us who have tried to keep together some semblance of organization for progressive democracy in Texas. . . ."

Despite her declining health, Frankie Randolph could not help but get involved when she felt her help was needed. She considered 1968 a pivotal year for Democrats and, as the election approached, wrote a letter encouraging them to get out the vote. "The Republican nominee [Nixon] and the third party candidate [Wallace] are dangerous threats to progressive government and lasting brotherhood among men," she wrote.

Senator Ralph Yarborough's defeat by Lloyd Bentsen, Jr., for the Senate seat he had held for so many years was a crushing blow to her, and she never hesitated in taking him to task for the loss. Yarborough wrote to her explaining that the press of Senate business had kept him in Washington, when he might have been in Texas campaigning.

He wrote to Randolph on June 19, 1970: "I only reached Texas . . . on the 17th day before the election. That day we spent in Galveston County. I went to the gates early in the morning at Monsanto Chemical Co. and the Union Carbide Co., the gates where thousands of workers pass through in a short length of time. Over half of them indicated hostility to my campaign, and I knew that we were in such deep trouble that it would be difficult to win. . . ."

Despite Randolph's continued interest in politics, the last years of her life were unhappy ones. Her angina led to her being bedridden for a year and a half, but she groomed her granddaughter Molly Luhrs to take up the mantle of active leadership in the Democratic party. With Billie Carr's help, Luhrs ran for precinct judge, campaigning door-to-door, but lost the race. Luhrs would remain active in the Harris County Democrats throughout the 1990s, until Carr's own declining health spelled the end of the group.

Luhrs reflected on her grandmother's influence on her own life and political involvement: "It was wonderful to have her as a mentor and role model. She really educated me, and made me feel I would be able to do things. I adored her with all my heart and soul."

In addition to her physical ailments, her marriage to Deke Randolph had deteriorated over the years. With their separate interests, they had gradually drifted apart, and with his wife's active involvement in politics, Deke had sought other female companionship. Randolph considered divorcing her husband, but family members, fearing that her angina, coupled with hardening of the arteries, was affecting her judgment, intervened to keep the couple together.

When Frankie Randolph died on September 5, 1972, obituaries defining her role in Texas politics appeared in major metropolitan newspapers across the state. Her family received a flood of expressions of sympathy—telegrams and letters from political colleagues and friends. The *Texas Observer*, the independent political journal she had helped build, also received notes and letters recalling her exploits. Friends and supporters, the people she had worked with through twenty years of an active political life, recalled their memories of her in rich and vibrant detail.

Writing in the *Houston Post*, Carr said of her mentor: "She was a heroine. I define heroism as that unique human quality that enables some of us to escape from our narrow world of self-interest to the wide world of common good. Mrs. Randolph had that quality and it fit her."

Gould Beech wrote: "She had a love of people—all people except those she believed were exploiting their fellowmen. . . . She could be gracious and lovable. But she could be tough. . . . She fused her life into the lives of many, who will not forget."

As a final salute to the journal's founder and financial backer, *Observer* editors Molly Ivins and Kaye Northcott editorialized: "Lady is a word not much in vogue in this feminist office, but comes a time when respect demands that word, with all its connotations of superiority. Frankie Randolph was a great lady; if to live a good and useful life, with rare style and integrity means anything, you will not forget that."

Few who knew her ever forgot Frankie Randolph. No one who worked with her ever forgot the fights she led and the progress she stood for. Certainly not the Harris County Democrats, who established their "Frankie" awards to honor public officials and workers who followed in her footsteps, or the editors of the *Observer*, who gave their Frankie Randolph Social Justice Award in her name. The Citizens' Education Association formed a policy center in her name, devoted to educating voters to participate in the governmental process. However, of all the honors, one she might well have esteemed above the rest was the creation of the Frankie Carter Randolph Park on Clear Creek, encompassing ninety acres of natural woodlands and green space in Harris County.

Part of the dream of County Commissioner Tom Bass, who was committed to developing a greenbelt, the parkland was designed to expand the county's green space and to help alleviate flooding. "Frankie's Park," as it was known, joined the Christia V.

Adair Park, honoring two remarkable women in Harris County's history who had joined together to work for civil rights. The park was dedicated on August 28, 1983, with Commissioner Bass, Ralph Yarborough, and Ronnie Dugger delivering memorial addresses.

Containing playgrounds, picnic and games space, but with forty acres of native plants and hardwood trees, the park was dedicated to Randolph's belief that "a community should provide parks and open spaces of natural beauty for all its people."

"Frankie's Park" was a fitting memorial to the girl from the pineywoods of East Texas, who had grown up among the pines, the cypresses, and the sweet gum trees, a young woman whose earliest memories were of Texas's most remarkable green space, itself, by the time of her death, part of the national preserve. It was fitting as well for a woman whose family fortune was made from the lofty East Texas pines, and one who made her mark on the politics of Texas and used her talents and fortune to work for social justice for all Texans.

For those who had worked with her, side-by-side in the turbulent world of Texas politics from the 1950s, her loss was a significant one. And it was in the pineywoods of East Texas that Billie Carr found her memories of Randolph most evocative: "She loved Camden, and when I go there and sit on her big back porch, I can feel her presence. It's just amazing how she left a mark on everyone she touched. I loved her dearly."

AFTERWORD

Legacy

The life of Frankie Randolph is one that encompasses not only interesting but also important years in the political life of Texas. She picked up the concerns of the loyalist Democrats of the 1940s and made them her own, harnessing the members of two groups, the Harris County Democrats and the Democrats of Texas, and carrying their members toward the implementation of a liberal agenda.

From the point of view of the 1990s, such goals as rescinding the poll tax seem minor, but to liberals during the 1950s and 1960s removing barriers so that every Texan had equal access to voting was not only important but mandatory. In the wake of Republican inroads into the politics of Texas, the loyalty oath seemed the only chance to preserve the Democratic party and to assure Democrats in elective office.

Each of her political comrades remembers her dedication, the sense of shared purpose they felt, the sense of community within the political life of the state that kept them fighting for liberal ideals. To many, Randolph was one of the members of that shared community who enlivened their sense of purpose and kept movements and issues energized.

In the liberal-labor movement, Randolph was a lodestar, a person who drew people to her, training them and empowering them to work toward a common goal—pushing issues, electing solid Democrats who worked for the liberal agenda, and seeing that every person had equal access not only to political office but to social justice as well. Her ability to work with the rank and file, as well as with leaders, endeared her to fellow liberals.

The political world of the 1950s was "a man's world," and she carved out a place in it, winning the respect and admiration of many of the male politicians. Sometimes they were a trial to her, and often she would tell Billie Carr: "Billie, you'll have to meet with 'the gents' . . . I'm tired of them." Yet, her support of "the gents" and her organizational skills helped send Ralph Yarborough to the U.S. Senate, Bob Eckhardt to the U.S. Congress, and Dean Johnston and Bill Kilgarlin to the Texas House of Representatives.

Her concepts of social justice, first learned from her mother and from her tutor, Willie Hutcheson, were indeed out of step with her times. Most Texans accepted segregation and discrimination; few worked to put an end to the status quo. She not only talked about ending segregation, but worked avidly toward that goal.

In the field of Texas women's political history, Randolph stands as a transitional figure, a woman activist who bridged the years between the "Petticoat Lobby" (the avid workers for suffrage, such as Jane McCallum and Minnie Fisher Cunningham) and the women who bombarded the electoral system in the 1970s and 1980s. Her money gained her access; her organizational talent ensured her place in history.

She learned from political women—"Minnie Fish," Lillian Collier, Marion Storm, and other activists—what women could do, and what they should do, and went about doing it in her own way, in her own time. In the Texas political world, she set the stage for Democratic women who followed in her footsteps by being the most active, certainly the most feisty, national committeewoman. She set the example and mentored women such as Billie Carr and granddaughter Molly Luhrs to carry on the "good fight," to keep the liberal agenda alive. Carr's greatest regret was that Randolph never lived to see her nominated and elected as Democratic national committeewoman.

Randolph's dedicated support of Barbara Jordan in her races for the Texas House and in her winning race for the Texas Senate was the capstone of her active political career. In her early political years, Randolph doubted whether women could win and serve in elective office in Texas. Jordan proved her wrong, and she became her most ardent advocate.

Her sponsorship of the *Texas Observer* alone would have won Randolph a place in the annals of Texas politics; but her allowing and encouraging the editors she hired to follow an independent course in the articles they chose to write and their writing itself was extraordinary. It won their lifelong respect and the respect of all those who work toward an independent journalism. The *Observer* remains a living testament to Randolph's ideals and the practical way in which she put her money to work where it would do the most good.

The editors of the *Observer* whom she worked with realized and acknowledged the uniqueness of her gifts to them, both her financial backing and their independence to write what they chose and how they pleased. Ronnie Dugger and Willie Morris, legends in the field of journalism, referred to her not merely in terms of respect and fondness—but also in terms of their love for her. Both Morris and Randolph's longtime political ally, Creekmore Fath, ranked her as "The Eleanor Roosevelt of Texas," and the accolade suits her.

Throughout her years in Texas politics, Frankie Randolph always stood by her convictions and fought the good fight. Hers was a life well worth living.

*N*otes

Notes are arranged by chapter and page number. The author's interviews for this book will form part of the Frankie Randolph Collection, Woodson Research Center, Fondren Library, Houston, Texas.

CHAPTER ONE—PINEYWOODS GIRLHOOD
page 1: Family members disagree as to what name FCR was given. Her sister, Agnese Carter Nelms, records the name as "Frank Maude," and FCR signed a number of letters as "Frank." Her birth certificate of record at the Polk County Courthouse, Livingston, Texas, records her name as "Frankie." Her nieces refer to her as "Aunt Frank," and "Maude" remains a family name within descendants of the Carters. For an overview of the East Texas pineywoods, see D. W. Meinig, *Imperial Texas*, and Mary Helen Hatchell Freeman, "East Texas: a social and economic history."

Stephen F. Austin quoted in Robert S. Maxwell and Robert D. Baker, *Sawdust Empire*, the best full-length coverage of the East Texas lumber business.

page 2: See *Sawdust Empire* and "East Texas: a social and economic history" for migration into East Texas.

For Andrew Smyth, see William Seale, *Texas Riverman*, pp. 67-75.

Mary Austin Holley quote from *Sawdust Empire*, p. 71.

For "sash saw" quote, see *Sawdust Empire*, p. 19. For an overview of the early East Texas lumber business, see *Sawdust Empire* and "Lumber: Early Polk County's Economic Lifeline." For a firsthand account, see John Henry Kirby, "The Lumber Industry of Texas."

page 3: "East Texas aristocracy" is an expression used by workers in the sawmills to refer to the timber barons and their families. Expression told to author by a lumber worker.

The founding of the Carter family lumber business is well documented; however, dates vary within sources. Best sources are *Sawdust Empire; J. Lester Jones, Centennial 1876-1976: W. T. Carter & Bro;* plus notes by Clarence Leon Carter in Frankie Carter Randolph Papers [private collection].

For the life and career of W. T. Carter, see "Men of Texas," p. 402; *Centennial 1876-1976: W. T. Carter & Bro.;* plus notes of Clarence Leon Carter.

page 4: For "great beauty," see notes by Agnese Carter Nelms in Frankie Carter Randolph Papers [private collection].

For "Maude, you know you tricked me. . . . ," see notes by Agnese Carter Nelms.

For "the finest investment. . . ," see "Men of Texas," p. 402.

For "Willy. The children and I . . . ," see notes by Agnese Carter Nelms.

For the building of the new mill, see *Centennial 1876-1976: W. T. Carter & Bro.;* plus notes of Clarence Leon Carter.

page 5: For Camden as a company town, see *Centennial 1876-1976,* plus "Many Communities Now Just Names, Memories," 7E; plus Joe Murray, "This Town Is Going to Die," 1:28 and "Camden: the last of the East Texas Logging Towns," p. 5.

For railways and East Texas logging, see Robert Maxwell, *Whistle in the Piney Woods: Paul Bremond and the Houston, East and West Texas Railway.* For Carter and railroading, see George C. Werner, "Texas Mixed: The Moscow, Camden, and San Augustine," pp. 7-16.

page 6: For "Mr. Carter's and Sid Adams's . . . ," see Werner, "Texas Mixed," p. 9.

For East Texas tourist attractions and Engine No. 5, see Frank X. Tolbert, "Disneyland has Little on Camden," 14.

pages 6–7: Agnese Carter Helms details in her notes the lives of the Carter children, their activities and social life during each season of the year.

page 7: For "fields of endeavor" and "social conscience," see notes by Agnese Carter Helms. Helms comments on the role that Maude Holley Carter took in developing the social conscience of her children.

For "responsibility of helping people less fortunate . . . ," see notes by Agnese Carter Helms.

page 8: All quotes regarding Agnese and Jessie from notes by Agnese Carter Helms.

For "get fair play . . . ," see notes by Agnese Carter Helms.

CHAPTER TWO—FROM HOUSTON HOYDEN TO SOCIETY MATRON

page 9: For W. T. Carter and his work in the mills, see *Centennial 1876-1976* and notes by Clarence Leon Carter in FCR Papers [private collection].

For "always a keen, interested sawmill man . . ." and "sweat on his brow. . . " see *Centennial 1876-1976.*

For an overview of Houston as a Texas rail center and port, see David McComb, *Houston: The Bayou City,* pp. 92-106.

The Carter home on Main Street is pictured in Marguerite Johnston's *Houston: The Unknown City, 1836-1946,* p. 151. Johnston's book chronicles the social life and changes in the lives of Houstonians during these pivotal years in the city's growth.

page 10: For W. T. Carter as businessman and King Nottoc XII, see *Centennial 1876-1976.*

For "watch out for any mistakes . . . ," see notes by Agnese Carter Nelms.

The Carter enclave at Courtlandt Place is well-documented. For descriptions of their houses, including the house where Frankie Carter spent her teenage years and lived as a young married woman, see *Houston: The Unknown City*, p. 131; "Beautiful Courtlandt Place"; "Heritage of Courtlandt Place," 2; "Courtlandt Place had Carter compound," 5.

page 11: For Frankie Carter's rebellious attitude, see author's interviews with Billie Carr and Molly Luhrs.

For a description of Willie Hutcheson, see *Houston: The Unknown City*, pp. 107; 185; 406n.

For Willie Hutcheson's influence on Frankie Carter's sense of social justice, see author's interviews with Billie Carr and Molly Luhrs.

For notes on American history, see Frankie Carter's ledger book in FCR Papers [private collection].

For W. T. Carter and Woodrow Wilson, see "Men of Texas," p. 402.

page 12: For Frankie Carter and the automobile, see interview with Molly Luhrs. For Houston's love affair with the automobile, see *Houston: The Unknown City*, pp. 149-155.

For Frankie Carter and the episode in Hermann Park, see interviews with Molly Luhrs and Billie Carr.

For Frankie Carter and the Baptist Church, see Billie Carr, "Fond Memories of Mrs. Randolph," p. 14J.

For the No-Tsu-Oh Carnival, Frankie as queen, and the end of the carnival, see "All Readiness for Houston's Jubilee," and *Houston: The Unknown City.*

page 13: For comment on FCR and "fancy dress," see interview with Molly Luhrs.

For Frankie's meeting with Robert Decan Randolph, see interview with Molly Luhrs and "Randolph Pioneered in U.S. Naval Air Corps," 6:6.

For Jane Randolph and Marguerite Radclyffe Hall's love affair, see Sally Cline, *Radclyffe Hall: A Woman Called John*, p. 44-45, 51.

For "perfect figure, lovely hands and feet . . . ," see *Radclyffe Hall*, p. 44.

pages 13–14: For Deke's visit with Radclyffe Hall, see interview with Molly Luhrs.

page 14: For Deke Randolph's adventures in World War I, see "Randolph Pioneered in U.S. Naval Air Corps," 6:6.

For anecdote concerning Frankie, Mike Hogg, and Deke Randolph, see *Houston: The Unknown City, 1846-1946*, pp. 205-206.

Telegram from Frank to Deke, June 7, 1918, in FCR Papers [private collection].

For "looks madder than hell," see interview with Molly Luhrs.

For Deke Randolph's business career, see "Randolph Pioneered in U.S. Naval Air Corps," 6:6 and brochure in FCR Papers [private collection].

page 15: For "simple, convenient, one-level house," see Charlotte Phelan, "Mrs. Randolph Is Controversial and Dedicated Person," p. A-14. [As society editor of the *Houston Post*, Charlotte Phelan kept FCR in the news, detailing her political activities and her lifestyle in the society section. In 1973, while interviewing the author, Phelan suggested that AFC look into the political careers of both FCR and Minnie Fisher Cunningham.]

For FCR's role in the founding of the Junior League, see Junior League folder, Texas Room, Houston Public Library. For "I don't know what a Junior League is . . . ," see Phelan, "Mrs. Randolph Is Controversial . . . ," p. A-14.

For "train debutantes to combine . . . ," see "You've Come a Long Way, Baby" article on Houston Junior League in FCR Papers [private collection].

For "he had all the room . . . ," and "nobody ever made money . . . ," see Phelan, "Mrs. Randolph Is Controversial . . . ," p. A-14.

page 16: For FCR as a golfer, see "Houston Country Club Golfers . . . ," p. 2-1.

For "rode his gaited horse . . . ," see *Houston: The Unknown City*, p. 317.

pages 16–17: For FCR and her nieces, see *Houston: The Unknown City, 1846–1946*, pp. 262-263.

page 17: For "She was just so much fun . . . ," see *Houston: The Unknown City*, p. 263.

For "a killing" and "quit the races," see Phelan, "Mrs. Randolph Is Controversial . . . ," p. A-14.

CHAPTER THREE— GOING FORWARD

page 18: For Junior League building, see Deed of Trust in FCR Papers [private collection].

For Patio Shop, see interview with Molly Luhrs.

For FCR and Georgina Williams, see interview with Molly Luhrs.

page 19: For FCR and the Citizens Charter Committee, see Spinks, "Titled Texan: Liberalism Just Simple Progress . . . ," p. 14.

For Houston and the city manager form of government, see Jewell, "The City Manager Plan," p. 13.

page 20: "Liberalism to me . . . ," see Spinks, "Titled Texan: Liberalism Just Simple Progress . . . ," p. 14.

For an overview of Minnie Fisher Cunningham's political activities, see "Mrs. Democrat: Minnie Fisher Cunningham" in Crawford and Ragsdale, *Women in Texas*, pp. 213-229.

For " 'Minnie Fish' could turn on . . . ," see interview with Bernard Rapoport.

page 21: For a detailed look at the issues of the Rainey firing and his campaign for governor, see Dugger, *Our Invaded Universities* and Carleton, *A Breed So Rare*.

For an overview of the politics of the period, see Green, *The Establishment in Texas Politics* and Key, *Southern Politics in State and Nation*.

For the Texas Regulars, see Weeks, *Texas Presidential Politics in 1952*, pp. 7–8.

For the Women's Committee on Educational Reform, see "Mrs. Democrat: Minnie Fisher Cunningham" in Crawford and Ragsdale, *Women in Texas*.

For opposition to the CIO in Texas, see *The Establishment in Texas Politics,* pp. 103-104, passim.

For *Sweatt v. Painter,* see Green, *The Establishment in Texas Politics,* p. 90.

page 22: Johnson's 1948 race against Coke Stevenson is well documented. For Johnson's rise to power in Texas and New Deal politics, see Caro, *The Years of Lyndon Johnson: The Path to Power* and the second volume, *Means of Ascent.*

For an overview of John Connally's role in Johnson's campaign, see Crawford, *John B. Connally: The Making of a Governor,* pp. 133-145; also Crawford and Keever, *John B. Connally: Portrait in Power.*

For organized labor's opposition to Johnson, see Green, *The Establishment in Texas Politics,* pp. 112-117; also interview with Chris Dixie.

pages 22–23: For the "tidelands" issue, see Hardeman, "Shivers of Texas," p. 53; also Green, *The Establishment in Texas Politics,* pp. 142-147.

page 23: For the "cowbarn Democrats," see Hardeman, "Shivers of Texas," pp. 8-9; also Kathleen Voight interview.

For Shivers and the labor-loyalists, see Hardeman, "Shivers of Texas," p. 53; also Green, *The Establishment in Texas Politics,* pp. 135-150; also interviews with Chris Dixie, Creekmore Fath, and Kathleen Voight.

For ". . . If he [Shivers] ever once says . . . ," see letter from Fagan Dickson to Walter Hall, Box 12, Walter G. Hall Papers.

page 24: For Rayburn and the Loyal Democrats of Texas, see Voight interview.

For the loyalists' bolt, see Voight interview, also Weeks, *Texas Presidential Politics in 1952,* pp. 16-25.

For "Who will go with me to La Villita?," see Voight interview.

For "Lord, help them . . . ," see "My Friends," *Texas Observer* (May 21, 1957): 1.

For the changes in the loyalist delegation, see Voight interview.

page 25: For Maverick and Harry Truman, see Voight interview; for the Maverick delegation at the Chicago convention, see brief in Walter G. Hall papers, July 21, 1952, Box 12; also Creekmore Fath interview; also Green, *The Establishment in Texas Politics,* pp. 145-146.

For "horrified" and "I don't even want that fellow . . . ," see Voight interview.

CHAPTER FOUR—FIGHTING FOR ADLAI AND RALPH

page 26: For "I'm Frankie Randolph . . . " see interview with Eddie Ball; also Charlotte Phelan, "Frankie Randolph, a Junior League Founder," A-2.

For "permanent organization . . . ," see Ball interview

For "We fussed and feuded . . . ," see Ball interview.

page 27: For "I set her up . . . ," see Ball interview.

For "rose through . . . ," see Ball interview.

For labor and African Americans within the loyalist-liberal movement, see interviews with Eddie Ball and Chris Dixie.

For "the leadership of the CIO . . . ," see Ball interview.

page 28: For Frankie Randolph and her crisis of conscience, see interviews with Ball and Dixie.

For "As an organizer . . . ," see Ball interview.

For liberals and Yarborough, see interviews with Ball, Dixie, Fath, and Voight.

For an overview of Ralph Yarborough's races against Allan Shivers, see "Shivers-Yarborough Shootout" in Green, *The Establishment in Texas Politics;* also D. B. Hardeman, "Shivers of Texas: a tragedy in three acts."

page 29: For "He didn't come on the scene . . . ," see Ball interview.

The Buchanan Dam meeting was an important organizing step in building the loyalist base in Texas. See interviews with Ball, Dixie, and Fath; also Rogers, "Historical Description and Analysis of 'The Democrats of Texas,'" pp. 14-16.

page 30: For Stephen Mitchell's admonition to the DOC, see Rogers, "Democrats of Texas," p. 16.

For "scuttle the DOC . . . ," see Ronnie Dugger, "DOC, DAC, and DOT," p. 2; also interview with Fath.

For "When we went to get the money . . . ," see interview with Ball.

pages 30–31: For contributions of wealthy Texans, see Green, *The Establishment in Texas Politics,* p. 163.

page 31: For coverage of the Shivers-Yarborough campaign, see Green, "The Shivers-Yarborough Shootout, 1954," in *The Establishment in Texas Politics* and D. B. Hardeman, "Shivers of Texas."

For an overview of the "red scare," in Texas, see Don Carleton, *Red Scare.*

For "an unwarranted invasion . . . ," see Green, *The Establishment in Texas Politics,* p. 156.

For Yarborough's stand on segregation and "genuinely equal," see Green, *The Establishment in Texas Politics,* p. 156.

page 32: For an overview of the influence of "The Port Arthur Story," and "ghost town," see Green, *The Establishment in Texas Politics* and D. B. Hardeman, "Shivers of Texas."

For the results of the Shivers-Yarborough campaign, see Green, "The Shivers-Yarborough Shootout," pp. 163-166.

CHAPTER FIVE—FOUNDING THE *TEXAS OBSERVER*

page 33: For an overview of the founding of the *Texas Observer,* see Franklin Jones, Sr., "The birth of the *Observer,*" pp. 28-29 and Carleton, *A Breed So Rare,* pp. 450-453.

For "I agreed to ask our board . . . ," see Jones, "The birth of the *Observer,*" p. 28.

For Jubal R. Parten's contributions to the *Texas Observer,* see Carleton, *A Breed So Rare,* pp. 450-452.

page 34: For ". . . hack political organ . . . ," and "If ever a rattlesnake . . . ," see Dugger, "Dugger remembers," p. 28.

For Bob Eckhardt's feelings about the newspaper and political candidates, see Dugger, "Dugger remembers," p. 28; also Bob Eckhardt interview.

For "who was introduced to me," see Dugger, "Dugger remembers," p. 28.

For "It was not so much . . . ," see Jones, "The birth of the *Observer*," p. 29.

For "She was the best . . . ," see Billie Carr interview.

page 35: For "Let me say candidly . . ." and "We need a newspaper . . . ," see draft of letter from Ronnie Dugger, January 17, 1960, in FCR Papers [private collection].

For board of trustees of the *Observer*, see "New Paper's Trustees Meet for first Time," p. 7.

For Randolph as treasurer of the *Observer*, see *Observer* file in Frankie Carter Randolph Papers [private collection].

For "The horrors of the transition . . . ," see Jones, "The birth of the *Observer*," p. 29.

For "to claim the loss . . . ," see Letter from R. H. Bentley to FCR, December 16, 1957, FCR Papers [private collection].

For "Mrs. Randolph from the beginning . . . ," see Dugger interview in Frankie Carter Randolph papers, Box 7, Woodson Research Center.

page 36: For "Mrs. Randolph trusted me . . . ," see Dugger interview in Frankie Carter Randolph papers, Box 7, Woodson Research Center.

For "Most of what I have to say . . . ," and "bring new ideas . . . ," see Draft of Letter from Ronnie Dugger, January 17, 1960 in FCR papers [private collection].

For "This is a free paper . . . ," see Morris, *North Toward Home*, p. 201.

For "the Eleanor Roosevelt of Texas," and "Some old ladies . . . ," see Morris, *North Toward Home*, p. 201.

page 37: For "Would you rather . . . ," see Fath interview.

For "I loved Mrs. Randolph," see Morris letter to author.

For "minimum wage . . . ," see Morris, *North Toward Home*, p. 249.

For "that obstreperous and . . . ," see Jones, "The birth of the *Observer*," p. 29.

For "journal of free voices," see masthead of the *Texas Observer*.

For "Until 1955 . . . ," see Morris, *North Toward Home*, p. 203.

page 38: For "A young reporter. . . ," see Morris, *North Toward Home*, p. 213.

For "delivered the *Observer* . . . ," "Kaye ran a tight ship," and "gave us laughter," see "Dugger remembers," p. 29.

For Molly Ivins's years on the *Texas Observer*, see Crawford and Ragsdale, "Molly Ivins—Having It All," *Texas Women: Frontier to Future*, pp. 323-331, and interview with Ivins.

For "the best job in American journalism" and "I loved working . . . ," see Ivins interview.

For "Some people think . . . ," "graduate school" and "You study . . . ," see Ivins interview.

page 39: For Bernard Rapoport and his support of the *Observer*, see interview with Rapoport; also Steven Long, "Observing Texas," *Houston Chronicle*, p. 5-D.

For "free journalism," see various comments by Ronnie Dugger.

For "serve no party . . . ," see masthead of the *Texas Observer*.

For *Observer* benefit party, see Nene Foxhall, "Observer's family reunion," *Houston Chronicle*, p. 13, and Long, "Observing Texas," 1-D.

For Yarborough and Frankie Randolph Social Justice Award, see Foxhall, "Observer family reunion," p. 13.

CHAPTER SIX—"KNOW WHO YOU'VE GOT AND WHO YOU'RE GONNA GET"

page 40: For the organization of the Harris County Democrats, see interviews with Chris Dixie and J. Edwin Smith.

For "Anybody who wanted to come in . . . ," see interview with Dixie.

pages 40–41: For "soon occupied an unofficial . . . ," and "I like her , . . ," see Dixie interview.

page 41: For Frankie Randolph's precinct organization techniques, see interviews with Ball and Dixie.

For "fast learner," "this task is impossible" and "Ralph's going to be there . . . ," see Dixie interview.

For "You've got to know who you've got and who you're gonna get," see Dixie interview.

For "got in the backseat . . . ," see Dixie interview.

For "Frankie was wonderful . . . ," see Fath interview.

For "Frankie had great intellect . . . ," see Ball interview.

For the organization of the Democratic Advisory Council, see Rogers, "Historical Description and Analysis of the 'Democrats of Texas,' " pp. 21-23; also Green, *The Establishment in Texas Politics*, pp. 172-174.

page 42: For the organizational meeting of the DAC, see Rogers, "Historical Description and Analysis of the 'Democrats of Texas,' " pp. 21-23.

For the organizational goals of the DAC, see interview with Creekmore Fath.

For FCR and Estes Kefauver, see interview with Chris Dixie.

For "She was completely dedicated . . . ," see interview with Eddie Ball.

pages 42–43: Randolph saved many articles, reports, and clippings that she read during this period. Many are in the FCR Papers [private collection].

page 43: For the Wednesday Club, see Barbara Karkabi, "Hattie Mae and Mary's Friendship brought people together." *Houston Chronicle* (September 17, 1989):1-C.

For "it always pained her to see . . . ," see Gould Beech letter, FCR Papers, Woodson Research Collection.

For "He's as unique . . . ," see Fath interview.

page 44: For FCR and train travel, see Fath interview.

For FCR and Camden, see interviews with Molly Luhrs and Maude Lenoir Carter.

For FCR and "rip the flesh," see interview with Luhrs.

CHAPTER SEVEN—LOCKING HORNS WITH LYNDON

page 46: For an overview of the events of 1956 and the conventions from the view of the loyalists, see Green, *The Establishment in Texas Politics*, pp. 171-174; also Carleton, *A Breed So Rare*, pp. 467-472.

For "favored a weekend romance . . . ," see *The Establishment in Texas Politics*, p. 172.

For the labor-loyalists and Sam Rayburn, see interviews with Ball, Dixie, and Voight.

page 47: For "rode in splendor . . . ," see interview with Voight.

For "I think we ought . . . ," "You have to be able . . . ," and "But Frankie and I made a deal . . . ," see Voight interview.

For "She had control . . . ," see Voight interview.

page 48: For "Lyndon threw a fit . . . ," and "We were not going to let . . . ," see interview with Eddie Ball.

For Johnson and Randolph's confrontation, see Ball interview.

For Johnson and J. Edwin Smith's confrontation, see Ball and Smith interviews.

For "J. Ed if you pursue this . . . ," see Ball interview.

For "J. Ed squared his shoulders . . . ," see Ball interview.

page 49: For "had to go tell . . . ," see Ball interview.

For "Womanpower for Eisenhower," "Do You Want . . . ," and "This turned the tide . . . ," see Ball interview.

For Parten's suggestion, see Carleton, *A Breed So Rare*, p. 469.

For Johnson's suggestions to Voight, see interview with Voight.

For Voight's pledge to Randolph and "run out of the state . . . ," see Voight interview.

For Andrews's and Hall's nomination of Randolph, see "Mrs. Randolph Elected to National Committee," *Houston Post* (May 23, 1956): p.1:1.

page 50: For "I could never thank...," see "Mrs. Randolph Elected...," p.1:1.

For "We won the battle . . . ," see E. L. Wall and Walter Mansell, "Loyalists Jubilant as Mrs. Randolph Nominated," *Houston Chronicle* (May 25, 1956): 1–1.

For "Well, Ed, you won . . . ," and "I had to go . . . ," see Ball interview.

For "favorite-son delegate . . .," see Ball interview.

page 51: Kathleen Voight commented to author "Lyndon gave and he took . . . ," after taped interview.

For "They threw us out . . . ," see interview with Billie Carr.

page 52: For Parten's protests to Rayburn and Johnson, see Carleton, *A Breed So Rare*, 472.

For "Mister, you're making the biggest mistake . . . ," see Carleton, *A Breed So Rare*, p. 472.

For Parten's feelings concerning Johnson and the liberals, and "red hots," see Carleton, *A Breed So Rare*, pp. 472-473.

For Randolph at the national convention, and "pretty much ignored Lyndon," see Fath interview.

For "carried a chip on her shoulder . . . ," see Ball interview.

For "Who gave you permission . . . ?" see interview with Billie Carr.

CHAPTER EIGHT—ORGANIZING THE DEMOCRATS OF TEXAS

page 53: For an overview of the founding of the Democrats of Texas, see

Rogers, "Historical Description and Analysis of the 'Democrats of Texas.' " The *Texas Observer* also carries details of each of the meetings of the steering committees and various issues important to the group. For "pretty much in charge...." and "good deal of political power ...," see Ball interview.

For Ralph Yarborough's final campaign for governor and his winning campaign for the U.S. Senate, see William G. Phillips, *Yarborough of Texas,* pp. 38-48 and Elton Miller, "The Yarborough Story," *Texas Observer* (October 16, 1964): 1-3.

page 54: For "We must elect ... ," see press release, Box 8, Frankie Carter Randolph Papers, Woodson Research Center.

page 55: For the "gut Yarborough" move in the Texas House of Representatives, see Green, *The Establishment in Texas Politics,* pp. 180-182.

page 56: For "... Through one campaign after ... ," see Carleton, *A Breed So Rare,* p. 475.

For "Mrs. Randolph's support ... , see letter from Yarborough, Box 8, Frankie Carter Randolph Papers, Woodson Research Center.

For "A great victory ... ," see "Tenacity Prevails," *Texas Observer* (April 9, 1957): p. 1.

page 57: For "try to intimidate ... ," see "New Protest Filed on Anti-Randolph Reports," *Houston Post* (January 15, 1957): 1-1.

For "It's a goddam lie" and "I have no comment," see Carpenter, "Democratic Bigwigs Hastily Deny Plan for Ouster of Mrs. Randolph," *Houston Post* (January 8, 1957): 4:8.

For "totally untrue" and "no one on the ... ," see Press Release from Mrs. R. D. Randolph, Box 3, FCR papers, Woodson Research Center.

For planning committee, see "'DOT' Plans Convention," *Texas Observer* (February 19, 1957): 7.

For Creekmore Fath's plan for the organization of the DOTs, see Rogers, "Historical Description and Analysis of the 'Democrats of Texas,' " also interview with Fath.

For "to work for the platform ... ," see "'DOT' Meets Saturday," *Texas Observer* (May 14, 1957): 1.

For "If DOT is nothing else ... ," see "Statehouse Control," *Texas Observer* (May 9, 1957): 2.

page 58: For "the greatest ... ," see "'My Friends,'" *Texas Observer* (May 21, 1957): 1.

For "a new force ... " and "developed directly from ... ," see Ronnie Dugger, "DOT Enters 'Heavy Class'," *Texas Observer* (May 21, 1957): 1.

For "We're going forward ... ," see Dugger, "DOT Enters Heavy Class," p. 1.

For the DOT insignia and its newsletter, see "DOT Expands Plans: Price Spurs His Troops," *Texas Observer* (June 14, 1957): 6.

For Eckhardt cartoon "Don't look now ... ," see "DOT's News Letter Views 'Safety Chain," *Texas Observer* (September 14, 1957): 7.

For "No Nickles for Pickle," and "no funds would be ... ," see "DOT: 'No Nickles for Pickle' SDEC: 'Harmony'," *Texas Observer* (September 20, 1957): 1.

page 59: For the feud between DOT and the SDEC, for "a serious rift . . . ," and for "was fighting for three rights . . . ," see "DOT-SDEC Feud Heats Meeting," *Texas Observer* (September 27, 1957): 5.

El Paso Times editorial quoted in "DOT- SDEC Feud Heats Meeting," *Texas Observer* (September 27, 1957): 5.

For background on J. J. "Jake" Pickle and Syres, Pickle & Winn, plus "extremists," see "SDEC Scores DOT 'Leftists'," *Texas Observer* (June 28, 1957): p. 8.

For "the same old Dixiecrat machine . . . ," "has always been a henchman for . . . ," "The state . . . committee . . . ," and "sponsor a party registration bill . . . ," and "They fear us . . . ," see "Pickle a New Target," *Texas Observer* (September 20, 1957): 4.

page 60: For Creekmore Fath and abolishing the poll tax, see interview with Fath. For "goofed," "published erroneous information," "subversion of democracy," " . . . betrays either gross stupidity . . . ," and Frankie Randolph's views on the DMN poll-tax story, see "DOT Catches Poll Tax 'Goof'," *Texas Observer* (November 20, 1957): 5.

For "I'm going to fight for you . . . ," see "Mrs. Randolph Nixes Johnson," *Texas Observer* (December 13, 1957): 4.

For "uncorked an unequivocal disapproval" and "It is criminal of any person . . . ," see "DOT Leader, Lyndon Feud Over Health," *Texas Observer* (December 13, 1957): 1.

page 61: For "prayers that sustained me . . . ," see "DOT Leader, Johnson Feud Over Health," *Texas Observer* (December 13, 1957): 1.

CHAPTER NINE—"TUGBOAT ANNIE" OF TEXAS POLITICS

page 62: For "Frankie Randolph is keenly . . . ," see letter from Walter G. Hall to Paul Butler, December 17, 1957 in Box 17, Walter G. Hall Papers, Woodson Research Center.

For "I want him to know . . . ," see letter from Walter G. Hall to FCR, December 17, 1957 in Box 17, WGH Papers.

page 63: For "junking the forty-hour . . . ," see "Letter to LBJ Scores Stand," *Texas Observer* (January 3, 1958): 1.

For "fine working force" and Johnson's reply, see "Letter to LBJ Scores Stand," *Texas Observer* (January 3, 1958): 1.

For "Our relative recent disdain . . . ," see "Letter to LBJ Scores Stand," *Texas Observer* (January 3, 1958): 1.

For labor's participation in the DOT, see Rogers, "Historical Description and Analysis of the 'Democrats of Texas,' " p. 70.

For General Preston Weatherred's warnings, see Lyman Jones, "Pundit of the Texas Right," *Texas Observer* (January 17, 1958): 1.

page 64: For "close ranks . . . ," "wipe from the Texas . . . ," and "Then would come repeal . . . ," see "Weatherred Warns Conservatives Again," *Texas Observer* (January 31, 1958): 1.

For Governor Daniel's opposition to the "Code of Ethics," see Rogers, "Historical Description and Analysis of the 'Democrats of Texas,' " p. 71.

For "Tugboat Annie" and "Dimpled Darling," see Sam Wood and Raymond Brooks, "Capitol A—Ladies Night," *Austin American* (January 23, 1958): A-1.

For "Frankie's letter to . . . ," see Letter from Walter G. Hall to Creekmore Fath, January 23, 1958), Box 17, WGH Papers.

page 65: For "I don't believe . . . ," see "Marietta vs. Frankie," *Texas Observer* (January 17, 1958): 1.

For "Ladies Night," "conservative . . . ," and "In the woman's world," see Wood and Brooks, "Capital A—Ladies Night," *Austin American* (January 23, 1958): A-1.

For "let's be ladies," and "I am a Democrat . . ." see Ronnie Dugger, "SDEC vs. DOT," *Texas Observer* (February 7, 1958): 4.

page 66: For "DOT . . . is not authorized . . . ," "If they're not . . . ," and "Indeed not . . . ," see "SDEC vs. DOT," *Texas Observer* (February 7, 1958): 4

For "has plagued the senator," see "LBJ/Frankie chat," *Texas Observer* (January 3, 1958): 1.

page 67: For "Johnson quite likely . . . ," see "LBJ/Frankie chat," *Texas Observer* (March 7, 1958): 4.

For "truly represented . . . ," "Republicans and Dixiecrats," and "Republican Price Daniel," see "Who's DOT," *Texas Observer* (April 11, 1958): 5.

For " . . . I do not believe . . . ," see "Who's DOT," *Texas Observer* (April 11, 1958): 5.

For Wharton County Democrats and their call for FCR to run for governor, see *Texas Observer* (April 25, 1958): 4.

CHAPTER TEN—VICTORY AT THE PRECINCTS

page 68: For the role of the Harris County Democrats and their legislative campaign in 1958, see e-mail letter from Bill Kilgarlin to author, May 18, 1999.

page 69: For backgrounds on legislative candidates, see e-mail letter from Bill Kilgarlin to author, May 18, 1999.

For " . . . her work in organizing . . . ," see e-mail letter from Bill Kilgarlin to author, May 18, 1999.

For the DOT second annual convention, see Rogers, "Historical Description and Analysis of 'The Democrats of Texas,' " pp. 72-77.

page 70: For "should not be linked . . . ," and for "Once we win . . . ," see "DOT: To Endorse Or Not?" *Texas Observer* (May 16, 1958): 8.

For "All I want . . . ," see "DOT: To Endorse Or Not?" *Texas Observer* (May 16, 1958): 8.

For " . . . were concerned that if DOT . . . ," see "DOT: To Endorse Or Not?" *Texas Observer* (May 16, 1958): 8.

For "political manipulation" and "sowing the seeds of disunity," see "DOT Attack Let Go By Governor," *Austin American* (May 29, 1958).

page 71: For "front for the DOT"; "Kingpin of the DOT"; and "ultraliberal Latin voters," see Ronnie Dugger, "The Sam Wood Story," *Texas Observer* (June 5, 1959):3.

For "racist propaganda . . . ," see "Daniel Charged in Use of Racist Progaganda, *Houston Chronicle* (July 7, 1958): 2:1.

For the DOT stance on endorsement, see Rogers, "Historical Description and Analysis of 'The Democrats of Texas,' " pp. 75-77.

For "with electrifying results" and ". . . DOT would have been bold . . . ," see "DOTs Convention," *Texas Observer* (June 6, 1958): 2.

pages 71–72: For "trying to create the impression . . ." and "locally, lawfully selected . . . ," see Letter to DAC members, Box 8, Frankie Carter Randolph Papers, Woodson Research Center.

page 72: For ". . . Let this much be understood . . . ," see Letter to DAC members, Box 8, Frankie Carter Randolph Papers, Woodson Research Center.

For "an outlaw minority group" and "could not get along . . . ," see "Price Hits Labor," *Texas Observer* (July 11, 1958): 8.

For the results of the Harris County legislative races, see e-mail letter from Bill Kilgarlin to author, May 18, 1999 and "Liberals Sweep Houston Runoffs," *Texas Observer* (August 29, 1958): 1.

For "This is the victory . . . ," see Al Hicken, "Liberals Carry Houston," *Texas Observer* (August 8, 1958): 1.

For the Texas Manufacturers Association and its Harris County Taxpayers Committee, see "Houston Liberals Score Grand Slam," *Texas Observer* (August 1, 1965): 1.

page 73: For ". . . the Harris County Democrats . . . ," see Letter from J. Edwin Smith to author, September 28, 1995.

For Governor Daniel's keynote speech, see Rogers, "Historical Description and Analysis of the 'Democrats of Texas,' " p.83.

For Daniel's manipulation of the SDEC, see "Moment of Bliss," *San Antonio Light* (September 11, 1958), clipping in Box 17, Walter G. Hall Papers.

For convention adjournment, see "Moment of Bliss," *San Antonio Light* (September 11, 1958).

For "ruthless, cynical . . . ," see "Moment of Bliss," *San Antonio Light* (September 11, 1958).

For the change of the DOT name to DOTC, see "DOT Becomes DOTC," *Texas Observer* (October 17, 1958): 4.

CHAPTER ELEVEN—"THE HARDEST WORKING DEMOCRAT"

page 74: For efforts to remove Randolph as national committeewoman, see "Move On to Oust Mrs. Randolph," *Houston Post* (September 13, 1956): 1:12; Carpenter, "Democratic Bigwigs Deny Plan for Ouster of Mrs. Randolph," *Houston Post* (January 8, 1957): 4:8; also Duckworth, "Move to Oust DOT Head Foreseen by Convention," *Dallas Morning News* (August 24, 1958).

For the controversy over Randolph and funds from the Democratic campaign dinner, see Carpenter, "Democratic Bigwigs Hastily Deny . . . ," 4:8.

For Randolph's support of Hattie White and "under the table," see interview with Chris Dixie.

page 75: For White's candidacy and "first time blacks and whites . . . ," see Barbara Karkabi, "Hattie Mae and Mary's Friendship brought people together," *Houston Chronicle* (September 17, 1989): 1-C.

For White's thanking Randolph, see Dixie interview.

For "Mrs. Randolph has done . . . ," see Creekmore Fath, "Report to Steering Committee of DOTC," in Walter Hall Papers, Box 12, Woodson Research Center, Rice University.

For resolution being "drawn," see Duckworth, "Move to Oust . . . ."

For Randolph's warnings against the FIA and "very few people . . . ," see Robert A. Baskin, "No Harmony Seen By Mrs. Randolph," *Dallas Morning News* (December 6, 1958).

page 76: For Randolph's feelings on Johnson's candidacy and "Lyndon has said . . . ," see Baskin, "No Harmony Seen By Mrs. Randolph."

For Johnson's entry into the 1960 presidential race, see O. Douglas Weeks, *Texas in the 1960 Presidential Election*, pp. 16-17.

For Johnson's dual candidacy, see Weeks, pp. 18-19; also e-mail letter from Bill Kilgarlin to author, April 5, 1999.

For the effects of liberal votes on the laws affecting Johnson's candidacy and "Because of Mrs. Randolph's . . . ," see e-mail letter from Bill Kilgarlin to author, April 5, 1999.

page 77: For Crooker's asking for a pledge from Woodrow Seals, see e-mail letter from Bill Kilgarlin to author, April 5, 1999.

For "There was no way . . . ," see Fath interview.

For "What can I do for you . . . ," see Carr interview.

For "liberal nominee . . . ." and "The nominee must not be . . . ," see "Party Politics: Two Preludes," *Texas Observer* (September 25, 1959): 1.

For Johnson's "two-time" loser, see "Views on Adlai," *Texas Observer* (October 30, 1959): 1.

For Walter Hall's opinion on Stevenson, see "Views on Adlai," p. 1.

For "I'm a Stevenson woman . . . ," see "Views on Adlai," p. 1.

page 78: For Randolph's listing as a "Texas Democrat for Stevenson," see "Views on Adlai," p. 1.

For "Creek, this is nonsense . . . ," see Fath interview.

For "battle for survival," "Conservatives have vowed . . . ," and "out of step," see "Move on to Oust Mrs. Randolph," 1:12.

For Truman's visit to Texas, "greatest living Democrat," and "You know what they say . . . ," see "DOT Decides 'Play It Cool,'" *Texas Observer* (October 23, 1959): 3.

pages 78–79: For G. Mennen Williams's visit to Texas, "liberal and dynamic," and "He is a super . . . ," see "Liberals Praised by Gov. Williams," *Houston Chronicle* (November 16, 1959).

page 79: For FCR receiving the Good Citizenship Citation; for "performed great public service . . . ," and "maintained . . . ," see "Mrs. Randolph Defended," *Texas Observer* (November 6, 1959): 1.

For Ralph Yarborough's speech; "by far the hardest . . . "; and "one of the tough years . . . ," see "Mrs. Randolph Defended," p. 1.

For "the greatest Democratic . . . ," "Not only has she . . . ," "join Frankie Randolph . . . ," see "Mrs. Randolph Defended," p. 1.

For the meeting of the DOT, "This year can be . . . ," and "you loyal DOT . . . ," see Walter Mansell, "D.O.T. Pledges National Dem Party Loyalty," *Houston Chronicle* (February 20, 1960): 2-1.

For Yarborough's letter and "June Democrats becoming . . . ," see "D.O.T. Pledges National Dem Party Loyalty," 2-1.

page 80: For Mullinax's resolution, see "DOT Lists Issues," *Texas Observer* (February 26, 1959): 1.

For labor's defection from the DOT, see Weeks, pp. 28-29; also "Johnson Scored, But Labor Not a Party," *Texas Observer* (May 20, 1959): 3; also "DOT Stance of Johnson Delayed," *Texas Observer* (May 20, 1959): 1; also Vernon Fewell, "Texas Labor Breaks with D.O.T. Wing," *Houston Chronicle* (August 8, 1960): 1:1.

For "not to mention. . . ." and "most annoyed . . . ," see "DOT Lists Issues," p. 1.

For ". . . You will go on fighting . . . ," see "Johnson Scored, But Labor Not a Party," p. 3.

For ". . . Texas labor's leadership . . . ," "Texas liberals . . . ," and "either the Texas liberals oppose . . . ," see "DOT and Johnson," *Texas Observer* (May 30, 1959): 2.

For ". . . Johnson has a good voting record . . . ," see "Johnson's Record Defended," *Texas Observer* (May 30, 1959):1.

page 81: For "A lot of conservatives . . . ," see "DOT Pledges National Dem Party Loyalty," p. 2-1.

CHAPTER TWELVE—DEFEAT

page 82: For statistics on the Ramsey-Yarborough race, see O. Douglas Weeks, *Texas in the 1960 Presidential Election.* Weeks's study remains the best source for the politics of the 1960 election in Texas.

For Randolph and the SDEC, see "Party Funds Rally 'Forgotten'," *Texas Observer* (March 25, 1960): p. 3.

pages 82–83: For the SDEC and the loyalty oath, see "The DOTC Pledge" in Weeks, *Texas in the 1960 Presidential Election,* pp. 17-18; for Billy Goldberg and Walter Hall's petitions, see Rogers, "Historical Description and Analysis of the 'Democrats of Texas,'" p. 103.

page 83: For "Frankie Randolph's latest . . . ," see Rogers, "Historical Description and Analysis of the 'Democrats of Texas,'" p. 104.

For battles in precinct and county conventions, see Weeks, *Texas in the 1960 Presidential Election,* pp. 20-24; also various articles in the *Texas Observer* (May 26, 1959).

For Travis County precinct fights, see Weeks, *Texas in the 1960 Presidential Election,* p. 22; also "Loyalists Lose Austin Roll Call on Stuart Long," *Texas Observer* (May 26, 1959): 1.

For Bexar County precinct fights, see Weeks, p. 21; also "Lyndon-Liberal Trade Prevails in San Antonio," *Texas Observer* (May 26, 1959): 8.

For Harris County Democrats and their vote, see Weeks, p. 22; "Houston: F.I.A. Roars; Lyndon Pledge Nixed," *Texas Observer* (May 26, 1959): 1.

For Randolph's loss in her precinct, see Weeks, p. 23.

page 84: For the loyalist vote and demands, see " 'On to Los Angeles— Mrs. R.'," *Texas Observer* (May 26, 1960): 1.

For "On to L.A." and "a good rumping group . . . ," see "On to Los Angeles—Mrs. R.'," p. 1.

For Randolph's demands and the liberal bolt, see "On to Los Angeles— Mrs. R.'," p. 1.

For Daniel's "wouldn't think" and his views on Randolph as national committeewoman, see "Daniel believes Mrs. R. Out," *Texas Observer* (May 27, 1960): 1.

For the DNC and loyalty resolutions, plus "It is understood . . . ," see Weeks, *Texas in the 1960 Presidential Election*, pp. 23-24.

page 85: For Johnson and the loyalty pledge, see Fagan Dickson, "Johnson Comprmises on Loyalty Pledge," *Texas Observer* (May 20, 1960): 4; also "Party Loyalty Issue Flares Up," *Texas Observer* (May 20, 1960): 5.

For labor and the loyalty oath, plus "goal we feel . . . ," see Weeks, pp. 25-29.

For Randolph's replacement as national committeewoman, see Weeks, pp. 25-29; also "Party Loyalty Issue Flares Up," p. 5.

For the Bexar County delegation's refusal to bolt, see Weeks, p. 25.

For "As you know . . . ," see Weeks, p. 26.

For "depleted and defeated," see Charlotte Phelan, "Frankie Randolph Leads Defeated DOT Back Home," *Houston Post* (June 19, 1960).

For "stubbornness . . . but unswerving," see Charlotte Phelan, "Frankie Randolph Leads Defeated DOT Back Home."

For the effects of the liberals' defeat at the state convention on the DOTC, see Rogers, "Historical Description and Analysis of the 'Democrats of Texas,'" pp. 103-105.

page 86: For "in Houston, Mrs. Randolph led . . . ," see Ronnie Dugger, "Dugger remembers . . . ," *Texas Observer* (January 14, 1977): 28.

For Randolph and Fath's box at the national convention, see Fath interview. For Johnson's opposition to Randolph's tickets and "I know one thing . . . ," see "Texas Delegation Circulates for Johnson," *Texas Observer* (July 15, 1960): 2.

For Randolph at the national convention, see Fath interview.

For "spreading the poison," see Dixie interview.

For liberals working the floor against Johnson, see "Texas Delegation Circulates for Johnson," p. 2.

For Daniel's stand on the national ticket, see Weeks, p. 26.

page 87: For Randolph's stand on the national ticket, see Carr interview.

For "really knew how to roll . . . ," see Carr interview.

For the HCD and "in carrying Harris County . . . ," see "Houston Bolt, Loyalists' OK Greet Kennedy," *Texas Observer* (July 22, 1960): 1.

For the Kennedy Ladies Tea, see Ann Staples, "The Liberals in Harris County and the 1960 Presidential Election."

For Kennedy's campaign trip to Texas, see Ronnie Dugger, "Texas Party Hierarchy Solid for Kennedy," *Texas Observer* (September 16, 1960): 5; also Staples, "The Liberals in Harris County and the 1960 Presidential Election."

page 88: For Randolph's ovation at the Houston City Coliseum, see Fath interview.

CHAPTER THIRTEEN—THE CONSCIENCE OF THE PARTY

page 89: For coverage of the Republican challenge to Democrats in 1961 and the Senate race, see John R. Knaggs, *Two-Party Texas*, pp. 1-15.

page 90: For Maverick's entry into the race and "For friends and associates . . . ," and "Maverick has firmer control . . . ,"see Ronnie Dugger, "Two Men Who Filled a Vacuum," *Texas Observer* (February 25, 1961): 5.

page 90-91: For statistics on the Blakely-Tower race, see Knaggs, *Two-Party Texas,* p. 9.

page 91: For the liberal dilemma, see Knaggs, pp. 10-12; also "Vote Stand Defended by Liberal Leader," *Houston Chronicle* (May 23,1961): 7-1.

For ". . . Blakely cannot be considered. . . ." and "I will do one or two things . . . ," see "Won't Vote for Either Senate Candidate, Mrs. Randolph Says," *Houston Chronicle* (May 23, 1961): 1; also Walter Mansell, "No Dems in Runoff Liberal Leader Says," *Houston Chronicle* (May 16, 1961): 1-1.

page 92: For Chris Dixie's vote on Tower, see Dixie interview. In *Two-Party Texas,* Knaggs asserts that Tower would not have made it to the U.S. Senate in 1961 without liberal votes.

For Connally's entrance into the Texas governor's race in 1961, see Crawford and Keever, *John B. Connally: Portrait in Power,* pp. 85-86.

For the race between Connally and Yarborough, see Crawford and Keever, pp. 85-93.

page 93: For ". . . Connally's candidacy . . . ," see Willie Morris, "Connally's candidacy," *Texas Observer* (December 15, 1961): 2.

For "surrounded himself with . . . ." and "a vote getting name . . . ," see Ronnie Dugger, "The Imminent Threat to Texas Liberalism," *Texas Observer* (January 19, 1962): 5.

For Randolph's support of Don Yarborough and "I'm going all out . . . ," see "We Can't Live Forever in the Past," *Texas Observer* (February 9, 1961): 1.

For the Wednesday Club, see Barbara Karkabi, "Hattie Mae and Mary's friendship brought people together," p. 1-C.

For Barbara Jordan's House races, see Crawford and Ragsdale, *Women in Texas,* pp. 322-323; also Rogers, *Barbara Jordan: American Hero,* pp. 86-90.

For an overview of the desegregation of Houston and race relations, see Chandler Davidson, *Race and Class in Texas Politics* and Thomas R. Cole, *No Color Is My Kind.*

For "She was very strong on civil rights . . . ," see Billie Carr interview.

page 94: For ". . . I went to the black YMCA . . . ," see Dixie interview.

For the work of the Houston Council on Human Relations, see Barbara Thompson Day, "The Heart of Houston: The Early History of the Houston Council on Human Relations, 1958-1972," *The Houston Review.*

For Jordan's defeat, see Rogers, *Barbara Jordan: American Hero,* pp. 88-90.
For Don Yarborough's loss to Connally, see Crawford and Keever, *John B. Connally: Portrait in Power,* pp. 91-93.
For Randolph's support of Eckhardt, see Bob Eckhardt interview.
page 95: For "You couldn't even get Eckhardt to campaign," see Carr interview.
For "Oh, my God . . . ," "Senator, this is Mrs. Randolph . . . ," "Billie, tell Mrs. Randolph . . . ," and "Nobody had a better . . . ," see Carr interview.

CHAPTER FOURTEEN—"SUCH AN INSPIRATION"
page 96: For "I went around the table . . . ," see Dixie interview.
For "We passed the resolution . . . ," see Dixie interview.
page 97: For Randolph's work with the Committee for Better Local Government, see Notes, Box 4, FCR papers, Woodson Research Center.
For liberal efforts to put members on the State Democratic Executive Committee, see Carr interview.
For Barbara Jordan's two House races, see "Congresswoman from Texas: Barbara Jordan" in Crawford and Ragsdale, *Women in Texas;* also Rogers, *Barbara Jordan: American Hero.*
For Jordan's endorsement by the Harris County Democrats, see Rogers, *Barbara Jordan: American Hero,* p. 104.
page 98: For the *Observer* endorsement of Jordan, see "A Question of Today," *Texas Observer* (April 29, 1966): 2.
For "We would say . . . ," see Carr interview.
page 99: For anecdote concerning Randolph and Cora Guerin, see Luhrs interview.
For anecdote concerning contretemps at Rudi's, see Luhrs interview.
For "When she came into a room . . . ," "She had wonderful eyes . . . ," and "She also had . . . ," see Carr interview.
page 100: For telegram to Dean Johnston, see Frankie Carter Randolph Papers, Box 3, Woodson Research Center. For Randolph's comments on Carr winning precinct judge, see Carr interview.
For "She was one of a kind . . . ." and "It's okay for you . . . ," see Carr interview.
For Randolph's illness, see Luhrs interview.
For "The waiters would rush . . . ," see Carr interview.
For the Texas Organization of Liberal Democrats, see "Liberals in Texas To Meet In Houston," *Texas Observer* (October 15, 1965): 1.
For letters to Latane Lambert and Warner L. Brock, and for "looking at his record," see Frankie Carter Randolph Papers, Box 3, Woodson Research Center.
page 101: For "go to the Piney Woods . . . ," see "Mrs. Randolph Plans 'Political Showdown'," *Houston Post* (August 23, 1965). Both the Randolph papers in the Woodson Research Center and the private collection contain numerous letters, articles, and speeches sent to Randolph by Yarborough.

For Randolph's recommendation of Bill Ballew, see Letter to Ralph Yarborough, August 17, 1965, Box 3, FCR papers, Woodson Research Center.

For Yarborough and his opposition to four-year terms for Texas governors and "Again your early leadership . . . ," see Letter, Yarborough to Randolph, November 11, 1965, Box 4, FCR papers, Woodson Research Center.

For Randolph's recommendation of Ed Cogburn, see Letter to Ralph Yarborough, August 15, 1966, Box 3, FCR papers, Woodson Research Center.

For comments on Cogburn's nomination and ". . . We loyal Democrats . . . ," see Letter to Randolph from Ralph Yarborough, August 15, 1966, Box 4, FCR papers, Woodson Research Center.

For ". . . The Republican nominee . . . ," see Letter to Liberal Democrats from Randolph, Box 3, FCR papers, Woodson Research Center.

page 102: For Yarborough's comments on his loss to Bentsen and the Senate campaign and ". . . I only reached Texas . . . ," see Letter to FCR from Yarborough, June 19, 1970, FCR Papers [private collection]. This letter is one of the sources of Yarborough's private comments on the loss of his Senate seat.

For Luhrs's precinct judge campaign and "It was wonderful to have her . . . ," see Luhrs interview.

For comments on Randolph's marriage to Deke Randolph and her illness, see Luhrs interview.

For Randolph's obituaries, see FCR papers [private collection].

page 103: For "She was a heroine . . . see Billie Carr, "Fond memories of Mrs. Randolph," *Houston Post* (March 2, 1986): 14J.

For "She had a love of people . . . ," see Letter from Gould Beech to *Houston Post* (September 8, 1972) in FCR papers [private collection].

For editorial see "Mrs. R. D. Randolph," *Texas Observer* (September 22, 1972): 15.

For Frankie Carter Randolph Park, see "Frankie's Park," *Houston Post* (September 5,1983): 2B; also dedication program in FCR papers [private collection].

page 104: For "a community should provide parks . . . ," see "Frankie's Park," *Houston Post*, 2B.

For "She loved Camden . . . ," see Carr interview.

AFTERWORD: LEGACY

Comments on the liberals' commitment, sense of purpose, and community may be found in the interviews of Ball, Dixie, Fath, Rapoport, and Voight. Also comments made to the author by Fagan Dickson.

Bibliography

PRIMARY SOURCES

Interviews
Eddie Ball and Ann Fears Crawford, Lake Livingston, August 28, 1998.
Billie Carr and Ann Fears Crawford, Houston, May 18, 1955.
Chris Dixie and Ann Fears Crawford, Houston, April 17, 1998.
Former Congressman Bob Eckhardt and Ann Fears Crawford, Austin, May 26, 1995.
Lida Arnold Edmundson, George Anna Lucas Burke, and Ann Fears Crawford, Houston, June 18, 1998.
Creekmore Fath and Ann Fears Crawford, Austin, April 24, 1998.
Molly Ivins and Ann Fears Crawford, Austin, April 22, 1996.
Molly Luhrs and Ann Fears Crawford, Houston, July 15, 1995; Molly Luhrs and Maude Lenoir Carter, March 24, 1999.
Bernard Rapoport and Ann Fears Crawford, Waco, June 12, 1999.
J. Edwin Smith and Ann Fears Crawford, Houston, September 9, 1995.
Kathleen Voight and Ann Fears Crawford, San Antonio, February 13, 1999.

Letters
William Kilgarlin to Ann Fears Crawford, via e-mail, April 4–5, 1999.
William Kilgarlin to Ann Fears Crawford, via e-mail, May 18, 1999.
Willie Morris to Ann Fears Crawford, April 20, 1999.
J. Edwin Smith to Ann Fears Crawford, September 28, 1995.

Archival Sources
Carter Family. File. Texas Room. Houston Public Library.
Corporation Record Book. *East Texas Democrat* and *Texas Observer*. Loaned to author by Molly Luhrs.
Courtlandt Place File. Texas Room. Houston Public Library.
Minnie Fisher Cunningham Papers. Special Collections and Archives, University Libraries, University of Houston.

Fagan Dickson Papers, Woodson Research Center, Fondren Library, Rice University, Houston, Texas.

Walter G. Hall Papers, Woodson Research Center, Fondren Library, Rice University, Houston, Texas.

Frankie Carter Randolph Papers. Woodson Research Center, Fondren Library, Rice University, Houston.

Frankie Randolph File. The Center for American History, University of Texas at Austin.

Frankie Randolph File. Texas Room. Houston Public Library.

Houston Junior League File. Texas Room. Houston Public Library.

Staples, Ann. "The Liberals of Harris County and the 1960 Presidential Elections." Unpublished research paper in Frankie Carter Randolph papers, Woodson Research Center, Fondren Library, Rice University, Houston.

Private Collections. Frankie Carter Randolph Papers. Loaned to author by Molly Luhrs.

Theses and Dissertations

Crawford, Ann Fears. "John B. Connally: The Making of a Governor, 1917-1982." Ph.D. dissertation. Austin: University of Texas, 1976.

Dickenson, Martha Kay. "Electoral Behavior in Texas from 1944 through 1972." M.A. thesis. Denton: North Texas State University, 1973.

Freeman, Mary Helen Hatchell. "East Texas, a social and economic history of the counties east of the Trinity River, 1850-1860." M.A. thesis. Beaumont: Lamar University, 1976.

Rogers, Robert G. "Historical Description and Analysis of the 'Democrats of Texas.'" M.A. thesis. Houston: University of Houston, 1963.

Tucker, Leah Brooke. "The Houston Business Community, 1945-1965." Ph.D. dissertation. Austin: University of Texas, 1979.

SECONDARY SOURCES

Articles

"All Readiness for Houston's Jubilee," *Houston Daily Post* (November 8, 1914): 1.

"A Question of Today," *Texas Observer* (April 29, 1966): 2.

Baskin, Robert E. "No Harmony Seen By Mrs. Randolph." *Dallas Morning News* (December 6, 1958).

Bailey, Ernest. "Houston Demos Lose on Ouster, But Win on Mrs. Randolph." *Houston Press* (May 23, 1956).

———. "Mrs. Randolph Lashes Back at Gov. Daniel." *Houston Post* (July 11, 1957).

Baskin, Robert E. "No Harmony Seen By Mrs. Randolph." *Dallas Morning News* (December 6, 1958).

"Beautiful Courtlandt Place." Unidentified article in Frankie Carter Randolph Papers, Private Collection.

Beech, Gould. "Frankie Randolph." *Houston Post* (September 8, 1972).

Billingsley, Lyn. "Heritage of Courtlandt Place." *Houston Post* (May 17, 1965): 2.

Brooks, Raymond, and Sam Wood. "Capital A." *Austin American* (July 15, 1958).

"Camden's Old-Train Graveyard Is Taking on New Life." *Houston Chronicle* (July 15, 1963): 3:6.

Carpenter, Elizabeth. "Democratic Bigwigs Hastily Deny Plan for Ouster of Mrs. Randolph." *Houston Post* (January 8, 1957): 4:8.

Carr, Billie. "Fond Memories of Mrs. Randolph." *Houston Post* (March 2, 1986): 14J.

"Daniel believes Mrs. R. Out." *Texas Observer* (May 27, 1960): 1.

"Daniel Charged in Use of Racist Propaganda." *Houston Chronicle* (July 7, 1958): 2:1.

Day, Barbara T. "The Heart of Houston: The Early History of the Houston Council on Human Relations." *Houston Review* 8 (1986): 1-31.

"Democratic Bigwigs Hastily Deny Plan for Ouster of Mrs. Randolph." *Houston Post* (January 8, 1957): 4:8.

Dickson, Fagan. "Johnson Compromises on Loyalty Pledge." *Texas Observer* (May 20, 1960): 4.

"DOT Attack Let Go By Governor." *Austin American* (May 29, 1958).

"DOT Becomes DOTC." *Texas Observer* (October 17, 1958): 4.

"DOT Catches Poll Tax 'Goof'." *Texas Observer* (November 20, 1957): 5.

"DOT Decides 'Play It Cool'." *Texas Observer* (October 23, 1959): 3.

"DOT Expands Plans: Price Spurs His Troops." *Texas Observer* (June 14, 1957): 6.

"DOT Leader, Lyndon Feud Over Health." *Texas Observer* (September 20, 1957): 1.

"DOT Lists Issues." *Texas Observer* (February 26, 1959): 1.

"'DOT' Meets Saturday." *Texas Observer* (May 14, 1957): 1.

"DOT: 'No Nickles for Pickle; SDEC Harmony'." *Texas Observer* (September 20, 1957): 1.

"DOT's News Letter Views 'Safety Chain.'" *Texas Observer* (July 14, 1957): 7.

"'DOT' Plans Convention." *Texas Observer* (February 19, 1957): 7.

"DOTs Convention." *Texas Observer* (June 6, 1958): 2.

"DOT-SDEC Feud Heats Meeting." *Texas Observer* (September 27, 1957): 5.

"DOT Stance on Johnson Delayed." *Texas Observer* (May 20, 1959): 1.

"DOT: To Endorse Or Not?" *Texas Observer* (May 16, 1958): 8.

Duckworth, Allan. "Move to Oust DOT Head Foreseen by Convention." *Dallas Morning News* (August 24, 1958).

Dugger, Ronnie. "DOC, DAC, and DOT." *Texas Observer* (April 4, 1958): 1.

———. "DOT Enters 'Heavy' Class." *Texas Observer* (May 21, 1957): 1.

———. "On Mrs. Randolph." *Texas Observer* (May 23, 1956).

———. "Dugger Remembers." *Texas Observer* (January 14, 1977): 28.

———. "Texas Party Hierarchy Solid for Kennedy." *Texas Observer* (September 16, 1960): 5.

———. "The Imminent Threat to Texas Liberalism." *Texas Observer* (January 19, 1962): 5.

——. "The Sam Wood Story." *Texas Observer* (June 5, 1959): 3.

——. "Two Men Who Filled a Vacuum." *Texas Observer* (February 25, 1961): 5.

Duncan, Dawson. "Frankie Randolph, Liberal." *Dallas Morning News* (February 2, 1958).

Fewell, Vernon. "Mrs. Randolph Backs Maverick for Senate." *Houston Chronicle* (February 20, 1961): 1.

——. "Texas Labor Breaks with D.O.T. Wing." *Houston Chronicle* (August 8, 1960): 1:1.

Foxhall, Nene. "Observer's family reunion." *Houston Chronicle* (May 20, 1989): 13.

——. "Politics—Texas style" in *Texas* magazine. *Houston Chronicle* (July 3, 1983).

"Frankie's Park." *Houston Post* (September 5, 1983): 2B.

"Letter to LBJ Scores Stand." *Texas Observer* (January 3, 1958): 1.

"Liberals in Texas To Meet in Houston." *Texas Observer* (October 15, 1965): 1.

Long, Steven. "Observing Texas." *Houston Chronicle* (May 23, 1989): 2:1.

Hamm, Madeleine McDermott. "Courtlandt Place had Carter Compound." *Houston Chronicle* (September 24, 1979): 5.

Hardeman, D. B. "Shivers of Texas: a tragedy in three acts." *Harper's* magazine 213 (November 1956): 50-56.

Hicken, Al. "Liberals Carry Houston." *Texas Observer* (August 8, 1958): 1.

"Houston Bolt, Loyalists' OK Greet Kennedy," *Texas Observer* (July 22, 1960): 1.

"Houston: F.I.A. Roars; Lyndon Pledge Nixed." *Texas Observer* (May 26, 1959): 1.

"Houston Liberals Score Grand Slam." *Texas Observer* (August 1, 1958): 1.

Jewell, Larry. "The City Manager Plan." *Houston* (September 1942): 13.

"Johnson Scored, But Labor Not a Party." *Texas Observer* (May 20, 1959): 3.

"Johnson's Record Defended." *Texas Observer* (May 20, 1959): 1.

Jones, Franklin, Sr. "The birth of the *Observer*." *Texas Observer* (March 11, 1977): 28.

Jones, Lyman. "Party Code is Proposed." *Texas Observer* (September 20, 1957): 5.

——. "Pundit of the Texas Right," *Texas Observer* (January 17, 1958): 1.

Karkabi, Barbara. "Hattie Mae and Mary's Friendship brought people together." *Houston Chronicle* (September 17, 1989): 1-C.

Kirby, John Henry. "The Lumber Industry of Texas." *The New Encyclopedia of Texas* (1926): 32.

Lacey, Margaret. "Houston Country Club Golfers Share Memories." *Houston Post* (January 14, 1957): 2:1.

Landrum, Lynn. "Ethics in Conventions." *Dallas Morning News* (January 1, 1958).

"LBJ/Frankie chat." *Texas Observer* (April 11, 1958): 5.

"Letter to LBJ Scores Stand." *Texas Observer* (January 3, 1958): 1.

"Liberals Praised by Gov. Williams." *Houston Chronicle* (November 16, 1959).

"Liberals Reorganize as Democrats of Texas." *Houston Post* (May 19, 1957): 1:11.

"Liberals Sweep Houston Runoffs." *Texas Observer* (August 29, 1958): 1.

Long, Steven. "Observing Texas." *Houston Chronicle* (May 23, 1989): 2-1.

"Loyal Democrats Plan Organization for '56." *Texas Observer* (March 28, 1955): 1.

"Loyalists Lose Austin Roll Call on Stuart Long." *Texas Observer* (May 26, 1959): 1.

"Lumber: Early Polk County's Economic Lifeline." *Polk County Enterprise* (August 29, 1974): 1E.

"Lyndon-Liberal Trade Prevails in San Antonio." *Texas Observer* (May 26, 1959): 1.

Mansell, Walter. "D.O.T. Pledges National Dem Party Loyalty." *Houston Chronicle* (February 20, 1960): 2:1.

————. "No Dems in Runoff Liberal Leader Says." *Houston Chronicle* (May 16, 1961): 1:1.

"Many Communities Now Just Names, Memories." *Polk County Enterprise* (August 29, 1974): 7E.

"Marietta vs. Frankie." *Texas Observer* (January 17, 1958): 1.

Mathis, Jim. "Mrs. Randolph Shows No Temper, No Axes—But Many Principles." *Houston Post* (May 24, 1956).

Maxwell, Robert S. "The Pines of Texas: A Study in Lumbering and Public Policy, 1880-1930." *East Texas Historical Journal* 2 (Fall 1964): 77-86.

"Men of Texas." *The New Encyclopedia of Texas* (1926): 402, 425.

Miller, Elton. "The Yarborough Story." *Texas Observer* (October 16, 1964): 1-3.

"Moment of Bliss." *San Antonio Light* (September 11, 1958).

Morris, Willie. "Connally's candidacy." *Texas Observer* (December 15, 1961): 2.

————. "Houston's Superpatriots." *Harper's* magazine (October 1961). Reprint in FCR private papers.

"Move On to Oust Mrs. Randolph." *Houston Post* (September 13, 1956): 1:12.

"Mrs. Randolph Backs Maverick." *Houston Press* (February 28, 1961).

"Mrs. Randolph Defended." *Texas Observer* (November 6, 1959): 1.

"Mrs. Randolph Elected to National Committee." *Houston Post* (May 25, 1956): 1:1.

"Mrs. Randolph, Liberal Dem Leader Dies." *Houston Chronicle* (September 6, 1972).

"Mrs. Randolph May Face Party Committee Ouster." *Houston Post* (January 6, 1957).

"Mrs. Randolph Nixes Johnson." *Texas Observer* (December 13, 1957): 4.

"Mrs. Randolph Plans Political Showdown." *Houston Post* (August 23, 1965).

"Mrs. Randolph Urges Democratic Support for Maury Maverick." *Texas State AFL-CIO News* (February 1961).

"Mrs. R. D. Randolph." *Texas Observer* (September 22, 1972): 15.

Murray, Joe. "This Town Is Going to Die." *Houston Chronicle* (July 28, 1968): 1:28.

————. "Camden: the last of the East Texas Logging Towns." *Texas* magazine, *Houston Chronicle* (July 16, 1967): 5.

"My Friends." *Texas Observer* (May 21, 1957): 1.

"National Party Reactivates Democratic Advisory Council." *Texas Observer* (January 24, 1955): 1.

"New Papers' Trustees Meet for First Time." *Texas Observer* (December 13, 1954): 7.

"New Protest Filed on Anti-Randolph Reports." *Houston Post* (January 18, 1957) 4:12.

"'On to Los Angeles—Mrs. R'." *Texas Observer* (May 26, 1960): 1.

"Party Funds Rally 'Forgotten'." *Texas Observer* (March 25, 1960): 3.

"Party Loyalty Issue Flares Up." *Texas Observer* (May 20, 1960): 5.

"Party Politics: Two Preludes." *Texas Observer* (September 25, 1959): 1.

Phelan, Charlotte. "As a Democrat, Mrs. Randolph Is Controversial and Dedicated Person." *Houston Post* (May 29, 1960) A-14.

————. "Frankie Randolph: A Junior League founder, who became a scrapper in the tough world of Texas politics." *Houston Post* (September 15, 1972): A-2.

————. "Frankie Randolph Leads Defeated DOT Back Home." *Houston Post* (June 19, 1960).

"Pickle A New Target." *Texas Observer* (September 20, 1957): 4.

"Price Hits Labor." *Texas Observer* (July 11, 1958): 8.

"Randolph Pioneered in U.S. Naval Air Corps." *Houston Post* (October 18, 1956): 6-6.

"SDEC Scores DOT 'Leftists'." *Texas Observer* (June 28, 1957): 8.

"SDEC vs. DOT." *Texas Observer* (February 7, 1968): 4.

Spinks, Brian. "Titled Texan: Liberalism Just Simple Progress to Mrs. Randolph." *Houston Post* (June 10, 1956): 2-3.

"Statehouse Controls." *Texas Observer* (May 9, 1957): 2.

"Tenacity Prevails." *Texas Observer* (April 9, 1957): 1.

"Texas Delegation Circulates for Johnson." *Texas Observer*: 2.

Tolbert, Frank X. "Disneyland Has Little On Camden." *Dallas Morning News* (March 17, 1962): 1-14.

"Views on Adlai." *Texas Observer* (October 30, 1959): 1.

"Vote Stand Defended by Liberal Leader." *Houston Chronicle* (May 23, 1961): 7:1.

"Weatherred Warns Conservatives Again," *Texas Observer* (January 31, 1958): 1.

Werner, George C. "Texas Mixed: The Moscow, Camden & San Augustine." Article in Frankie Carter Randolph Papers, Private Collection, 7–16.

"Won't Vote for Either Senate Candidate, Mrs. Randolph Says." *Houston Chronicle* (May 23, 1961): 1.

"Who's DOT." *Texas Observer* (April 11, 1958): 5.

Wood, Sam, and Raymond Brooks. "Capitol A—Ladies Night." *Austin American* (January 23, 1958).

"W. T. Carter, Jr., Ex-Councilman, Financier Dies." Typescript of Newspaper Obituary in Frankie Carter Randolph Papers, Private Collection.

Books and Pamphlets

Adams, Ann. *Firestarter Files: The Public and Private Letters of Franklin Jones, Sr. 1981-1984.* Oak Harbor, Washington: Packet Press, 1985.

Bass, Jack, and Walter DeVries. *The Transformation of Southern Politics: Social Change and Political Consequence Since 1945.* New York: Basic Books, 1976.

Carleton, Don E. *A Breed So Rare: The Life of J. R. Parten, Liberal Texas Oil Man, 1896-1992.* Austin: Texas State Historical Association, 1998.

———. *Red Scare!: Right-wing Hysteria, Fifties Fanaticism, and Their Legacy in Texas.* Austin: Texas Monthly Press, 1985.

Caro, Robert A. *The Years of Lyndon Johnson: Means of Ascent.* New York: Alfred A. Knopf, 1990.

———. *The Years of Lyndon Johnson: The Path to Power.* New York: Alfred A. Knopf, 1982.

Cline, Sally. *Radclyffe Hall: A Woman Called John.* New York: Overlook Press, 1997.

Cole, Thomas R. *No Color Is My Kind: The Life of Eldrewey Stearns and the Integration of Houston.* Austin: University of Texas Press, 1997.

Crawford, Ann Fears, and Jack Keever. *John B. Connally: Portrait in Power.* Austin: Jenkins Publishing Co., 1973.

———, and Crystal Sasse Ragsdale. *Texas Women: Frontier to Future.* Austin: State House Press, 1998.

———. *Women in Texas: Their Lives, Their Experiences, Their Accomplishments.* Austin: State House Press, 1992.

Davidson, Chandler. *Race and Class in Texas Politics.* Princeton, NJ: Princeton University Press, 1990.

Dorough, C. Dwight. *Mr. Sam.* New York: Random House, 1962.

Dugger, Ronnie. *Our Invaded Universities: Form, Reform, and New Starts.* New York: W. W. Norton & Company, 1974.

———. *The Politician: the life and times of Lyndon Johnson.* New York: W. W. Norton, 1982.

Feagin, Joe R. *Free Enterprise City: Houston in Political and Economic Perspective.* New Brunswick, NJ: Rutgers University Press, 1988.

Fuermann, George. *Reluctant Empire: The Mind of Texas.* Garden City, New York: Doubleday & Company, Inc., 1957.

Green, George Norris. *The Establishment in Texas Politics: The Primitive Years, 1928-1957.* Westport, Conn.: Greenwood Press, 1979.

Gunther, Pete. *The Big Thicket.* Austin: Jenkins Publishing Co., 1971.

Henderson, Richard B. *Maury Maverick: A Political Biography.* Austin: University of Texas Press, 1970.

Johnston, Marguerite. *Houston: The Unknown City, 1836-1946.* College Station: Texas A&M University Press, 1991.

Jones, Eugene W. (ed.) *The Texas Country Editor: H. M. Baggarly Takes A Grass-Roots Look At National Politics.* Cleveland: The World Publishing Company, 1966.

Jones, J. Lester. *Centennial 1876-1976: W.T. Carter & Bro.,* rev. edition 1978. Privately printed. [Loaned to author by Maude Lenoir Carter].

Key, V. O., Jr. *Southern Politics in State and Nation.* New York: Vintage Books, 1949.

Kinch, Sam, and Stuart Long. *Allan Shivers: The Pied Piper of Texas Politics.* Austin: Shoal Creek Publishers, Inc., 1973.

Knaggs, John R. *Two Party Texas: The John Tower Era, 1961-1984.* Austin: Eakin Press, 1986.

Maxwell, Robert S., and Robert D. Baker. *Sawdust Empire: The Texas Lumber Industry, 1830-1840.* College Station: Texas A&M University, 1983.

———. *Whistle in the Piney Woods: Paul Bremond and the Houston, East and West Texas Railway.* Houston: Texas Gulf Coast Historical Association, 1963.

McComb, David. *Houston: The Bayou City.* Austin: University of Texas Press, 1969.

Meinig, D.W. *Imperial Texas: An Interpretive Essay in Cultural Geography.* Austin: University of Texas Press, 1969.

Morris, Willie. *North Toward Home.* Boston: Houghton Mifflin, 1967.

Phillips, William G. *Yarborough of Texas.* Washington, DC: Acropolis Books, 1969.

Pictorial History of Polk County, Texas, 1846-1910. Livingston, Texas: Heritage Committee of Polk County Bicentennial Committee and Polk County Historical Commission, 1978.

Rogers, Mary Beth. *Barbara Jordan: American Hero.* New York: Bantam Books, 1998.

Seale, William. *Texas Riverman: The Life and Times of Captain Andrew Smyth.* Austin: University of Texas Press, 1966.

Steinberg, Alfred. *Sam Rayburn: A Biography.* New York: Hawthorn Books, Inc., 1975.

Thomas, Richard D., and Richard W. Murray. *Progrowth Politics: Change and Governance in Houston.* Berkeley: Institute of Governmental Studies, 1991.

Weeks, O. Douglas. *Texas in the 1960 Presidential Election.* (Public Affairs Series Number 48.) Institute of Public Affairs. Austin: The University of Texas, 1961.

———. *Texas Presidential Politics in 1952.* (Public Affairs Series Number 16.) Institute of Public Affairs. Austin: The University of Texas, 1953.

Index